Arguments Against

The Early Religious Pamphlets of
Rev. B.H. Shadduck, Ph.D.

Edited by Brian J. Hunt

Introduction Copyright © 2010 Brian J. Hunt.
Jocko Homo label © 1977 Man Ray Inc.

In this facsimile edition some pages may
have been edited to improve visual clarity.
No content has been altered or omitted.

ISBN: 978-0-578-06623-3

First Edition: September 2010
10 9 8 7 6 5 4 3 2 1

www.bhshadduck.org

Published by GB Graphics

Table of Contents

7   Introductions

13   Jocko-Homo the Heaven-Bound King of the Zoo

49   Puddle to Paradise

89   The Toadstool Among the Tombs

125 The Gee-Haw of the Modern Jehu

161 Alibi, Lullaby, By-By

197 The "Seven Thunders" of Millennial Dawn

233 Rastus Agustus Explains Evolution

269 Pages From Later Editions

Rev. Bertram Henry Shadduck, PhD
April 14, 1869 - March 2, 1950

Born in Erie County, Pennsylvania, Rev. Shadduck stated he did not have a particularly religious upbringing, but used religion as an excuse to get out of farm work on Sundays. At the age of eighteen after hearing a sermon that changed his life, Rev. Shadduck joined the Salvation Army as a teacher in the schools the Army maintained for training officers. Six years later he met and married a former African missionary. After leaving the Salvation Army in 1894, he enrolled in a course of study with the West Virginia Conference of the Methodist Church where he distinguished himself and graduated with the highest honors. In 1902 he was ordained a deacon and quickly rose to elder status in 1904. Taking postgraduate work at the School of Philosophy at Grove City College, he received a Doctorate of Philosophy in 1912.

In 1923 *The Sunday School Times* published his anonymous testimony of his finding his faith. Following the success of his testimony he serialized the homespun minstrel-show humor of "Rastus Augustus 'Splains Evolution" over three issues.

That same year he wrote his first pamphlet **Jocko-Homo, The Heaven Bound King of the Zoo** (later editions were known more simply as **Jocko-Homo Heavenbound**). First advertised in *The Pentecostal Herald* in March of 1924, the first edition of 7000 copies sold out within twenty days. A second printing of similar size also quickly sold out.

In 1924 Rev. Charles Francis Potter of the West Side Unitarian Church and later adviser on the Bible to Clarence Darrow in his defense of John Thomas Scopes, declared that Sunday, April 27 would be "Evolution Day." The centerpiece of the celebration was the unveiling of a bronze by Carl Akeley entitled "Chrysalis". Rev. Potter maintained that the sculpture held "real spiritual message for men of today.... The point of the

Akeley's Chrysalis

statue is not the gorilla but the man, who has risen above his animal ancestry."

Travis

Responding to this, in the third edition of **Jocko-Homo Heavenbound**, Rev. Shadduck included a satirical sketch by his friend Rev. M. M. Travis of his version of "Chrysalis" as a frontispiece. This was to be later redrawn by F. W. Alden and moved to the cover. This was destined to become an iconic image.

Alden

The controversy over evolution would capture the attention of the nation in the 1925 Scopes-Monkey Trial. What started as a simple court case over a Tennessee law concerning the unlawful teaching of evolution became a springboard for the highly charged emotions on both sides of the issue. That same year Rev. Shadduck published two more anti-evolution pamphlets, **Puddle to Paradise** and **Toadstools Among the Tombs**.

In 1928 Shadduck published **Alibi, Lullaby, By-By** and **The Gee-Haw of the Modern Jehu**. Unlike his earlier works that attacked evolution directly, these new pamphlets took the faithful to task for not being more active in battling the theory of evolution.

Later in the same year he published **The "Seven Thunders" of Millennial Dawn**, a written expose' on the Jehovah's Witnesses where he used their own writings against them. Rev. Shadduck offered to debate the Jehovah's Witnesses but was never able to come to mutually agreeable terms of debate. On one occasion the opposing debater insisted that Rev. Shadduck put up a $500 bond against his slandering the Jehovah's Witnesses' literature in any way.* Fearing that the use of any quotes from the Jehovah's Witnesses' literature would be considered slander, the debate never happened.

* See page 203

Near the end of 1928 Rev. Shadduck reworked his Sunday School Times serial into the humorous pamphlet **Rastus Augustus Explains Evolution**. Shockingly politically incorrect by today's standards, Rastus is a black janitor at a college who overhears evolutionary theory during the course of his cleaning and comes home and debates it's merits with his wife Mammy Lou.

With the multiple reprint editions of his pamphlets and their increasing popularity, Rev. Shadduck became a much sought after public speaker at schools, churches, and other public forums all across the United states. He would not publish a new pamphlet until 1940, and those are the subject of another book.

Around 1970, Kent State University art students Gerald Casale and Bob Lewis met Mark Mothersbaugh, who introduced them to the pamphlet **Jocko-Homo Heavenbound**. One of the illustrations is of a devil with the word "D-EVOLUTION" on his chest.  This cartoon and many of the concepts in the pamphlet helped name and influence their fledgling musical group, *DEVO (The*  *D-Evolution Band)*. The B-side of their first 45 single in 1977 was the song "Jocko Homo". Lyrics include "They tell us that/We lost

our tails/Evolving up/From little snails". The concept of the evolutionary losing of tails is a common theme of ridicule in the cartoons of several pamphlets.

In this volume we present the first seven pamphlets of Rev. Shadduck. Whether you agree with the ideas of Rev. Shadduck or not, the sheer volume of pamphlets distributed attest to the weight his ideas must have had on the populace of the time.

Brian J. Hunt

GB Graphics

Arguments Against

JOCKO-HOMO

THE HEAVEN-BOUND KING OF THE ZOO

By B. H. SHADDUCK, Ph. D.
Rogers, Ohio.

SIXTH THOUSAND

PRICE 15 CENTS

PENTECOSTAL PUBLISHING COMPANY
LOUISVILLE, KENTUCKY

Arguments Against

TO DOUBTING BELIEVERS—MORE OR LESS.

The first edition of this book met with every sort of reception but one; no one known to the author, offered to refute it.

Some have complained that it showed scant courtesy to Christian evolutionists. I reckon every man my comrade, who accepts the whole Bible for what it claims to be. I harbor only love for any man who fosters no past or present insincerity. If you are not open to conviction and are a little gunshy, this is the place to lay the book down.

My father fed me on Darwinism and called it infidelity. To me, it was a blinding curse; now when the self-appointed committee on Bible renovation brings in the former outcast as a wet nurse for a mongrel theology, I remember that I have met the old "gal" before. I regret that I know of no way to heave a brick at the old squaw and seem perfectly polite to the enamored bystanders.

If you have an open mind or a willingness to expose the fallacy of this book, here are seven little questions for beginners.

1. If it were conceded that there were man-like animals before Adam and animal-like men after the fall, cross breeding and corruption of the race described in Genesis; how could that disprove that God made an image-man without proxy and forthwith?

2. Does evolution continue to function, so that we may some day develop horns, hoofs, shell, wings, gizzard, wheels or smokestack?

3. Ought it to continue so that the strong may crush the weak?

4. Among earth's teeming billions, is any creature developing a wart, wen, wrinkle, blister, freckle or pimple, into an organ or limb?

5. Why is it that 99.999999% of life continues in one cell form, in defiance of evolution?

6. What law would put a tail on a gobbler's nose and a whisk broom on his breast?

7. What law would handicap destructive creatures as does poison itch in the bite of blood sucking insects; (provoking destruction) or the 17 years of helpless infancy for "locusts"?

1

Arguments Against

PARENTS, PASTORS, EVANGELISTS, TEACHERS, SOLDIERS.

What most "modernists" least desire is to be WHOLLY UNDERSTOOD. What the confused world needs is a word husker that will reveal what clever phrases conceal. Take as a sample,—"What difference does the virgin birth make, anyhow?" Rub the fuzz off and it means,—"What difference does it make if the Bible does tell lies?" Back of pretty phrases that glorify lopsided love, is an unspoken denial of wrath and vengeance as possible to God. The smiling evasion of one miracle means that all must go when the dear public is educated up to it. If you doubt it, take a blue pencil and a Bible to a "modernist" and ask him to delete all that he does not accept as the Word of God without equivocation or mental reservation. Will he do it? He will not. **He works with the thin end of the wedge.** The true prophet always sees the big end of the wedge.

Millions are spent to advertise "Well's Relining of History," "Van Loon's Childish Stories" and other subtle attacks on the Bible. Other millions (including your money) support schools and preachers that substitute "the best modern thought" for revelation. The uncircumcised press brings the new universalism to your breakfast table as a finding no longer disputed by educated people.

Many books unanswerable in logic, defend the faith, but,—
   (a) They cost too much for wide distribution.
   (b) They are too lengthy for tired working people and busy students.
   (c) Their scholarly style is not readily grasped by common folk.

This little book is designed to meet a real need. If you think it will help the perplexed wayfaring man or the student who is being pried loose from home teachings, it is sold in quantities at cost.

One evangelist ordered 1,000. One college president sold them to his students.

"Modernists" do not agree. Drive them into the "open" and they will walk all over each other. Let doctrinal "pussyfooting" cease. SHELL THE WOODS!

2

JOCKO—HOMO
(Monkey Man)
THE HEAVEN BOUND KING OF THE ZOO.
BY B. H. SHADDUCK, PH.D.

LIBERALISM.

In all ages there have been people who found the religion of Jehovah not sufficiently *democratic* for their liking. God did not put his laws and his revelations to a *vote*. He did not consult them in making the original; they do not consult him in making the amendments. It is the history of all religions that men try to shape their lives to their faith or shape their faith to fit their ambitions and desires. Men who do not like a "meddlesome" God, find too much *iron* and not enough *rubber* in the Word of God for their comfort. The elaborate criticisms that add elasticity to revelation are now heralded under the labels of modernism.

RATIONALISM.

For centuries, another school of thought, making equal claim to scholarship and freedom from superstition has held the Bible up to mockery and ridicule, boldly proclaiming deliverance from its pall of ignorance and tradition.

DARWINISM.

Yet another school of thought arose and framed a theory that makes man the culmination of a selfish, merciless struggle that

3

Four

began with an invisible speck of life in the slime of the sea a billion years ago. This theory excused God from any direct and personal responsibility. For all they knew *or cared*, God is a myth and man an *accident*.

WHERE THREE STREAMS MEET.

It was inevitable that in time these three streams should flow together, and as in the case of rivers that unite, the currents of each keep to their own side of the valley *for a time;* so the drifting churchmen, in an effort to save their face and some of their faith, profess a separate identity and shy not a little at the crowd that goes with them. After robbing the infidel thinkers of their theory of ape relationship on which they had spent a life time, they tied the word *"Theistic"* on it, like a can on a dog's tail, that they may wean it and shoo it away from the company that it has been in. Their embarrassment is like that of the man who stole a pig and the old sow followed him home. As yet, they are uncertain how much responsibility for the process is to be put on God.

TRUTH IN THE SHOW WINDOW.

In every false teaching there is an element of truth. Certain well known facts are wrested from their logical connections and put in the *show window* and the credulous passer-by is easily deceived as to what the shop really turns out. We know, of course, that all creatures born or hatched are in

Five

form, habits and mentality, a blend in variable degrees of the contributions of all their ancestors. We know that in the selfish struggle for food, shelter and mates and against fire, famine, frost, flood and foe, ALL *must* perish and *some* will perish *first*. These are *show window* facts. What we protest against, is that back of the public display, in the department of speculation, they juggle with an eternity of time, an infinity of mystery and the infinitesimal of life and label the theories that are changed as many times as Jacob's wages,—"science." They agree on but one thing, that is the *predetermined* conclusion that one kind of creature may be transmuted into another kind.

SPECULATION OR REVELATION.

There is a modification of species recognized in the Bible and the barnyard. For all I know to the contrary, the oft repeated assertion that our horses developed from little horses, may be true; but when the evolutionary fairies put a marsupial sack on a reptile in one age and take it off in the next, in their efforts to make a man, I question the infallibility of human speculation rather than divine revelation.

Were there man-like races before Adam? I don't know. The Bible does not say there were not. *If there were*, they need not help and they could not hinder God in making his *image-man* as he says he did.

Six

Old bones only prove that brute races and families have passed and will pass. Rudimentary organs prove that equipment not used, be it a wing or a soul, becomes atrophied. THAT IS NOT EVOLUTION, it is the *opposite*. *It is going the wrong way.* Show us a species that is *coming* or an organ that is *in the making*. Show us how to grow wings where there are none.

Any false theory is half damned if stated in simple words. It is all damned if forced to be consistent. It is twice damned when you take off its parade uniform and make it work.

VERBAL SMOKE SCREENS.

Evolution means to *unroll*. Any schoolboy knows that the more you unroll a thing, the smaller it gets. The famous phrase,—*"The survival of the fittest,"* has for years been relied upon to explain the process of evolution. It sounds pretty, and seems pious, but what it really means is,—"Might makes right." "Dog eat dog." "Root hog or die." "The weak to the wall." With such a theory, "modernists" propose a compromise,—"Let us slip God in somewhere, and you may evolve the Bible also." The scholar who believes the "fact" of evolution, doubts the infallibility of the Bible. I know of no exception.

CHANGE OF FRONT.

If evolution was God's plan in the past, it

ought to be good now. If applied to society today, it would mean,—let the weaklings starve, eat your enemies, practice polygamy and encourage old people to die.

KALEIDOSCOPIC.

I am told that Darwinism has been abandoned and that I am fifty years behind the times in fighting it. I know it. The latest confessed scientist is ever chasing his predecessors off the stage. The next generation will make fun of what we now call science. That is why it is not really science.

TRUTH NOT AT WAR WITH TRUTH.

Now I do not resist any real science for a moment, nor do I find the Scriptures in conflict with any truth. By the Holy Scriptures, I mean the original writings accepted by Christ and his church. The old "chestnut" that the church resisted proof that the world is round, is neither analogous nor wholly true. When the circle of the earth was proven, the church looked for it in the Bible and found it there. Jesus clearly warned the world that when he comes, it will be night one place, daytime another place. That the earth is round, is easily demonstrated; that Eve was not made from a rib, never has been proven, and in the nature of the case never can be proven. Nor can it be shown that God did not make Adam from dust, without the help, permission or connivance of apes then or critics now.

Eight

ROMANS 11:34.

To know what God *did not* do is to know what he *could not* or *would not* do. You cannot settle a dispute over a line fence in an honest court without sworn testimony. Let those who would impeach the testimony of the Bible, be sworn.

"GOOD" AND "VERY GOOD."

We admit that Adam was made by the same maker, to eat, drink, and breathe the same elements and weather the same storms. We admit that he was meant to be an improvement on anything previously made. Genesis says God inspected his work and four times pronounced it "good." After that he made man and pronounced his work *"very good."* All the unidentified bones that were ever dug up or imagined could only show that God did not need to make a great change in his "good" to make his "very good."

THE FIRST CRITIC.

If all the brute markings that evolutionists are so eager to find in themselves, are conceded just to please the brotherhood, yet they can only show what man *is* since the fall, not what he was before "all flesh had corrupted his way upon the earth." According to Genesis, some creature called Nachash was "more subtle than any beast of the field that Jehovah God had made." I do not know who he was, nor what he looked like before he was cursed with serpent shape, but

Nine

he used language, posed as a critic of the Word of God, qualified as an educator and had a seed that made trouble for the Adamic race. If he had maintained a copyright on his philosophy, we should now be spared the claim that it is "modern" thought and "new" conception."

ALL FLESH CORRUPT.

Later, it is reported that visitors or neighbors who were not proper mates for the chosen race, intermarried with them to the great grief and anger of God. Even animals were involved in the fearful corruption of all flesh. "There were nephilim in the earth in those days." I do not know who any of these trouble makers were, but they may have left a few bones for the collectors to use in making an uncle or grandpa for Adam.

PAPER AND INK RACES.

With a bone, a belief and a bottle of ink, the confessed experts have peopled the prehistoric wilderness with bull-necked, fish-mouthed races that fit into the scheme as desired. They pause in their labors to deny that God could make even one lone man by himself. Verily when men begin to doubt the Bible, they believe what they wish to believe.

TESTIMONY OF THE DUST.

If evolution is true, man ought to be vastly improved physically, but man is the sickest thing on earth. If culture is what the

Ten

race needs, the schools ought to have vastly improved his morals, but poison gas, bombs, Bolshevism, Bohemianism, white slavery and birth control seem to thrive in civilization even better than in savagery. The dust of a thousand buried cities witness of man's experiments and mark the end of the trail that leads *from* the Garden of Eden.

AN ALIBI FOR SIN.

There is no logical place for inbred sin in evolution, hence its devotees have substituted the epigrams,—"if man ever fell, he fell upward." "The sin in the Garden of Eden was the effort of an ape to become a man." "God made man, but he used a monkey to gather the dirt." Such of the Bible as they cannot misconstrue to fit their fancy, they discredit by calling it "Hebrew Conception," "folk lore," "tribal psychology" and "the phantasmagoria of undeveloped minds." Sin, the stinking cancer and rotting leprosy of society, is called "arrested development." If there is a personal God, they admit he may be annoyed. Well's Outline of History says of a war-lord who drenched Europe with blood,—*"God was bored with him."*

WHAT WORRIES THE CRITICS.

The only trouble the critics have, who would save enough of the Bible for sick beds and funerals, is to decide where the blue pencil is to stop now that it is well started. If the God of Genesis is only a "tribal god," the God of John's gospel may be only John's

Eleven

notion of God. If the Garden of Eden is a myth, heaven may go to the scrap pile next. If the virgin birth is in doubt, the resurrection is under suspicion. If some miracles must go, which ones may stay? If the Bible is mistaken in telling us from whence we came, how can we trust it to tell us where we are going? How much will be left to assure the little mother with bent form and broken heart, that

> "In the morn those angel faces smile
> "Which I have loved long since and lost awhile."

Consistency is not to be expected of spoon-fed prophets who find the Bible must be skimmed, strained and diluted to fit their digestion, but to those who think through to logical conclusions, it is obvious that the dictator who will furnish God an alibi in Genesis, will have his resignation ready for him in Revelation. The unbelief that makes the first Adam a "sport," will not balk much if the second Adam is denied a legitimate birth. If each man may sift the Bible for himself and throw away anything which he thinks is Babylonian tradition, Rabbinical interpolation, Grecian influence and Pauline narrowness; *constitutional government will be next to go.* When the masses learn to sniff at the authority of the Word of God, they will snort at the authority of man-made laws. The critics shall yet be more anxious to stop the flood, than they were to start the leak.

Twelve

EITHER SIN OR EVOLUTION IS TO BLAME.

After the Nachash beguiled mother Eve with his "new theology," man tried to get away from God even as he does today. Later, the race took another plunge into depravity by some sort of cross breeding and God uses ten expressions in six verses, to record his grief, disgust and disappointment. There is no place in the story for metaphor to make it mean exactly the opposite from what it says. There is no room for exegetical fog on which to paint evolutionary rainbows. Either it is the truth or it is a pitiful palpable lie. If Bible embellishers can calmly survey the lust, treachery and hell of horror that has followed, and not see that something has happened to God's plan; if all the hideous nightmare of cruelty is only God's method of making a frog into an angel; then heaven is on the far side of hell and no detour. If for a thousand ages of inferno, there was only hate without mercy, brute force without pity, plunder without remorse, while God worked with his dirt; if in all the teeming wilderness, there was no prayer but the scream of terror, no answer but the hush of death as the jaws of the killer dripped with blood; is not the new theology overworking the love side of its religion?

DEVIL NEEDED TO EXPLAIN.

If there is no devil, there needs to be one to account for the overflowing deviltry of earth. If after all the committees on social

Thirteen

uplift have experimented for 6000 years with the mess the apes left on their hands and the most favored nation leads the world in crime, divorce, prizefighters, chorus girls, commercialized sport, cliques, dope and birth control; if with our university halos, a prize fight or a barbecue has ten times the drawing power of a bishop, isn't it about time to let the apes mix up another batch? In every display of samples of what evolution is doing for man in this decade, the system *backfires.* So far is it from God's plan that death shall be the twin angel of life and the brood mother of progress, that he says,—"The last enemy that shall be destroyed is death." When his kingdom comes; when the "prince of this world" is banished, God will restore Eden conditions and the "Lamb and the lion shall lie down together."

BUDDHISM FITS.

Buddhism is the only religion that fits evolution, for it proposes to breed *out* with a thousand reincarnations, what evolution says has been bred in on the journey from tadpole to man. Does it seem reasonable that God would take years as numberless as the stars to build the frail human body that goes back to dust in a few years, and then in the twinkling of an eye, "when they that are in the graves shall hear the voice of the Son of God," call it back to an endless life? Better the faith of ignorance than the folly of wisdom.

Fourteen

NEW CLOTHES FOR OLD THOUGHTS.

The miracles and "days of vengeance" in the Bible have always fretted the men who make programs for God. They would limit his power and tone down his wrath by exalting human reason above revelation. Of late, they would overawe us with a display of scholarship and rescue us from the "outworn portions" of the Bible. They have much to say of "new" knowledge and "freedom of thought." This heroic talk is, after all, but the remouthing of the "outworn portions" of Ingersoll, Paine and Voltaire. The only thing new about the movement that I can see is that the attack is *from the inside*. Every bloody handed anarchist who ever threw a bomb was for "unshackled thought" and freethinkers and freelovers can say amen. How often in life the masses are confused and "bunk" passes for heroics. What and where is this free thought? In all nature, that marvelous something or somewhat that we call instinct, guides the thoughts of the dumb creatures and guides them well. Among humans, it is well known that the mother imposes her thought characteristics upon the child *before it is born*. If she is a good mother, she determines in a great measure, the content, habits and direction of the child's thought after it is born. True freedom of thought would mean to be hatched in an incubator and kept solitary in a brooder the remainder of life. Even at that, instinct

Fifteen

and experience might force one's thoughts into certain channels. What are schools and teachers for, if not to amend and direct thought? Freedom of thought in school is about as practical as freedom of weeds in the garden. The freest thought in the world is that brought "into captivity to the obedience of Christ." (2 Cor. 10:5).

FREEDOM TO MOULD OTHER MINDS.

Any man may indulge in a veritable riot of thinking as he pleases and no one would be the wiser. The ones making the fuss about their freedom to think are the very ones most anxious to impose their thoughts upon others. What they really seek is freedom of propaganda. They wish to teach in schools and churches paid for and kept up by believers and shape plastic minds in moulds of unbelief. If some mariner wishes to abolish the stars and sail by a lantern that he hangs in the rigging, he may do so, but not with my boat or my boy. The hoax of the barnyard is the setting of duck's eggs under a hen. Even so, a man eager to make a stir in the world, may warm the imported eggs of rationalism and thenceforth ask only for freedom to cluck and scratch. A close observer may often know what professors a man studied under by *hearing him talk*. One may fairly guess the literature a preacher reads, by hearing his sermons. Sometimes I wonder if there may not be false parrots as well as false prophets. I freely confess regret for

Sixteen

originality. What I work out that is not wrought in by the Spirit, God send that it may be short lived. God grant that all who have been joined to Christ "that we might bring forth fruit unto God," (Rom. 7:4) may be spared the shame of incubating the eggs of some intellectual cuckoo. *God needs no one to do his thinking for him.*

IS IT TRUE?

The proclamation of independent thought has ever been the mark of the false prophet. The true prophet only relayed the message of God. Not even Christ claimed to speak his own thonghts. He who spake as never man spake, said, "I spake not from myself; but the Father that sent me, he hath given me a commandment, what I should say and what I should speak." (John 12:49). Already the church is topheavy with self-sufficient scholarship. We are well nigh powerless to stem the tide of worldliness, Sabbath desecration and commercialized sport. We could well afford to trade three schools for one Pentecost.

"HAIL MASTER."

We protest not against reason, but treason. Better a kiss from the moist lips of Judas than compliments from the fawning lips of a professed follower of Christ who is secretly bent on correcting the mistakes of Christ. It may be indeed, that they will substitute their own rags for his robes, but they shall never flag a hell-bent world, sex-mad,

Seventeeen

money-mad, sport-mad, with a shirt-tail Bible.

FOG, NOT FIRE.

Every philosophy of life must begin with something. The Scriptures begin with God and those who fear him, walk with unshod feet in a world of mystery, sure of nothing but revelation. Worldly wise men, with more self-reliance than all the prophets for 6000 years, light their wicks from each others' candles and forbid the darkness. Not with a "pillar of fire," but with a mantle of fog, they would bedim the light that God has set in the front door of the Bible to call sinning man back to innocence and Eden. They bid him forget that he has fallen and offer him what? A grave in the dark. What else can there be for an heirloom of the apes? Man is then, *only the little smear of primodial gravy that unrolled.* MONKO-HOMO, THE HIGHBROW, KING OF THE ZOO.

THE LOST MATTER AND FORCE.

Most evolutionists ask only for matter and force from which to evolve all earthly life. Not that they understand matter and force, or ever will, but the wayfaring man thinks we understand it and is therefore the more easily deceived. Any scholar knows that there are a dozen elements and as many manifestations of force, any one of which if missing, the earth would fall apart or become a desert. What the evolutionist wants (if he knows) is matter and force in a thousand

Eighteen

forms and combinations, nicely adjusted and *doing business* exactly as though there were a master mind directing it. Then he must have a special matter and force that will evolve *just one life* and then *disappear* forever. He will not tell you this and the joke is, that he may never have thought of it. You see if that particular matter and force should continue doing business for thirty minutes, it might evolve a whole flock of little ancestors and then we could never be sure we all came from the same pioneer. It is well understood that matter and force that can evolve life from dead matter is not working on earth now. It evolved just one little "dodad" and something shooed it away, else it might make an Adam when it acquired experience.

TOO MUCH FOR CHANCE.

An idiot working haphazard in a print shop would be as likely to set up Lincoln's Gettysburg speech by chance, as that blind matter and force could adjust themselves to the creation of just one life and furnish it with enough of that mysterious abstraction that men call "nature," so that it could divide with the swarming millions of earth's creatures and each have just enough and just the right kind.

THE BORROWED HAT.

Evolution has been likened to a magician who borrows a hat and before a wondering audience takes out of it only *what he puts*

Nineteen

into it. The show is a success because the spectators fail to catch him at the trick. Continuing the parable, the evolutionist makes a good showing by diverting your attention to something else, while he adds to his collection of wonders that he will presently take out of his theory. He will divert your attention to what he calls laws, till he slips *life* into the hat and then show you the life while he puts in the *laws*. Law begets life and then life begets laws. The first life is presumed to be so small that a billion of them could live in a thimble and very insignificant. Nevertheless it is life that no one but God understands, and without which God could not exist nor the universe be known. Little as it is, it has the greatest program thrust upon it of any life short of God himself. It must *unroll* till earth and sky and heaven and hell are full, *if faith and foolishness are twins.*

ABSTRACT LAW.

What is law? Darwin said it "is the observed sequence of events." It sounds profound, but no one was there to *observe* and there was no *sequence* of events until there were *two* events in the life of the inexperienced germ. If there could be two events in this first life without law, then law did not order the events. Unless logic is turned topsy turvy, that law was there waiting for life, or the life could proceed without the law. There is no law apart from a law giver

Twenty

any more than there is a bung hole without a barrel or a cipher with the rim knocked off. Something must provide instinct, appetite, food and digestion for the first life and it fools the wayfaring man to say, "law did it." If you inquire what there was to eat before either animal or vegetable life; law must take all responsibility.

STARTERS AND STOPPERS.

Fully equipped inside and out and able to get his own living, the first baby "ancestor" was infinitely better fixed than human babies who are the most helpless things on earth. That little "forefather" ought to have been satisfied and never have started something we have been quite unable to finish. If it had been content to hold its own, what a peaceful world this had been, but it introduced a revolution without precedent,—a miracle *if it happened but once*. It began to *grow*. It had no need to grow for it was meeting its environment perfectly. Besides, growth would in time make it so large that the earth would be lopsided. It must *stop* growing. Wonderful, that a *stopper* should come along at the right time. Then happened an event as wonderful as that which befell Adam; only when it happened to Adam, it couldn't happen because it was a miracle. The little invisible speck had a puckering in the middle and without any previous experience, it puckered itself in two. You may call it addition, sub-

Twenty-one

traction, multiplication or division, but *nothing unrolled.*

BEFORE HEREDITY ARRIVES.

Famous evolutionists say that the only factors in evolution are heredity, variety and environment. When a little invisible bubble of soup breaks in two, both ends are the same age and variety and both have the same environment. There is nothing that could put a tail on one end and horns on the other, and if there was, yet the immediate breaking in two would leave both ends crippled. Each half is the other end of the other half and never in eternity can evolution jump the gap between the cell without sex and parents, and the creatures of sex and parents. If sex gets started, some one must start it.

THE FIRST "ANCESTORS" REFUSE TO DIE.

Right here, the famous law of the survival of the fittest breaks down hopelessly. Even a half wit must see that according to this law, *anything that survives must be the fittest.* All about us are "squintillions" and "squidrillions" of one-celled germs just like the one that is presumed to have started the trouble. They are able to survive *where we cannot.* They can live in water, ice, air or dust, and for years at a time without food. Since they are the "survivingest" little survivors the world has ever known, then they are the fittest and nothing else had a license to survive.

Twenty-two

THE IMPASSABLE GULF.

Sex is a most necessary factor in the theory of evolution, but they cannot get it into life with any laws that they acknowledge. Their laws would *keep it out*. It could not come by accident, since the mental and material equipment necessary to each sex, would fill a catalog and a whole flock of accidents at the same time would be necessary. It could not help anything survive that *had been* surviving before, and *has been* surviving since. It would be a positive *handicap* to creatures that could multiply by merely breaking in two. Sex is an intricate maze of mystery that hides its puzzle beyond the barriers where human reason breaks down. What the unrollers need is a Santa Claus to bring it down the chimney, ready to function, with all its instincts, affinities, jealousies, penalties and rewards. Then, and not till then can the evolutionist bring his trick rules to bear. He cannot get what *he calls* his fittest, to survive until he gets it to *arrive*.

TRICK RULES.

"Only grandma can make me mind," said a willful child.

"How does grandma do it?"

"She tells me to do what she tells me, *or not*."

Thus the evolutionists have made their rules so that they will work three speeds ahead and *reverse*. If God Almighty was to make outright and forthwith, a new creature

Twenty-three

of flesh with bone or no bone, red blood, white blood, hot blood, cold blood; rig it out with electric lights, artillery, umbrella and any instrument in the orchestra; they would fence it in with rules and shoo it into their menagerie. Here are some of the rules abbreviated.

I. Be like your ancestors or be different.
II. The fittest shall survive and the unfit may live.
III. Grow big or stay little; either will help you to survive or not.
IV. That your family may survive, lay a million eggs or give birth to one.
V. Unused organs shall disappear or persist.
VI. Rudimentary organs are what you have had or what you will have.
VII. Win a mate by combat or not; it will help the family survive, or not.
VIII. Polygamy will help survival, unless you prefer to mate in pairs.
IX. Fight your neighbors or unite with them; one way or the other will help.
X. Wear gaudy colors or avoid display, so shall your family survive.
XI. Develop legs, wings, tail, horns, shells or not; they will help, or not.
XII. Do everything that in the far future, theorists say you have done.

WHAT UPSETS DARWINISM.

If the fairies or "Lady Luck" or the great god Jupiter will donate sex to sexless creatures, the birth, rearing and scattering of a family will, without doubt, modify within limits. With the family *taken* for granted, the mind that *takes* things for granted will not see the *fatal blunder* of letting the family business proceed recklessly. It must be personally conducted or destroy itself. The codfish is said to lay 10 million eggs and the

Twenty-four

elephant to give birth to one in 10 years, yet there are enough elephants and none too many codfish. If the birds of prey hatched 16 like the quail or many pairs each year like the pigeon, things would go to smash, for it is conceded that without worm eating birds, most life would speedily vanish from the earth. Some one must line up the parade. If the worms arrive five years ahead of the worm eaters, the earth will become a desert. Evolutionists say the worms arrived some millions of years ahead of the birds. The first worms may have been *good worms* and lived on scraps. All the *starters* and *stoppers* must get here at exactly the right time; must be numerous or few; must be long lived or short lived; just right to preserve the balance and ballast of things. If vegetation did not give off oxygen, if animal life did not give off carbon dioxide, no life would be possible. There is a germ called botulinus bacillus that produces a toxin, a spoonful of which is enough to destroy all human life. Fortunately it is more rare than yeast germs. The great monsters of prehistoric times have disappeared, to our great comfort. The reverent student of nature will thank God for holding evil in check now, even as he believes the promise that God will some day banish it.

THE DIZZY CIRCUIT.

With law, luck or lingo, the theorist explains everything. He can argue that cer-

Twenty-five

tain factors are the cause of evolution or that they are caused by evolution. It depends on which you wish explained. Like a dog chasing his tail, the dog makes the tail go and the tail makes the dog go, depending on which end of the dog you wish explained. It is the unwritten law of evolution that EVOLUTION WILL PRODUCE ANYTHING THAT WILL PRODUCE EVOLUTION.

REGISTERED STOCK.

There are several pedigrees thrust upon us by so-called science. I give below, the one prepared by the Jordon-Kellogg School because they are considered high authorities. I doubt not that there are others more recent and will be another one next year; all of them *temporarily* scientific.

READ UP.
Man
Anthropoids
Old World monkeys
Lemurs
Marsupials (like opossums)
Reptiles (related to 3 eyed lizards)
Amphibians (the frog family)
Lung bearinga fish (as the fringefins)
Sharks
Lamphrey or Lancet (something like an eel)
Worms
Hydra or Volvex. Hydra is like a piece of macaroni with spaghetti trimmings. Volvex resembles a ball of green jelly with whiskers.
Amoeba (able to project limbs from the body and withdraw them)
Plasm

Arguments Against

Twenty-six

By this list it is apparent that we had limbs aplenty and at will in the second chapter and exchanged them for quite other trimmings in the third. On the fourth floor we had worm legs which vanished on the fifth. Fins appeared during the fifth or sixth experiment and went out of style in the eighth. A swim-bladder came in style about the same time and went out about a million years ahead of the fins. We have had four kinds of a tail that has served as propeller, rudder, guy-rope, swing and hitching strap. If they will tell us what we *are to get* in the next distribution, a million years hence, we may forgive evolution for the mean tricks it has played on us.

ARE WE FITTER NOW?

Once we could live in water or on the land. Once we had cold blood and could winter in the cold mud without food. Once we could leave a case of eggs in the water or sand and let the census taker do the worrying. Later when warm blooded babies came in style, our marsupial mothers tucked them away in a large vest pocket and never a baby cried. Think of the good old days before handkerchiefs and soap were needed.

WHAT A FARMER BOY KNOWS.

The originator of the brotherhood explained some of the changes listed above by the sifting process of survival. In explaining the development of color and song in birds,

Twenty-seven

they adopt a *contrary* law. They presume that the female bird selected the mate with the color and song to her taste. It is characteristic of false theories that they *make* more problems than they solve. Where would the lady bird get such fastidious tastes? Why should lady black birds all take a fancy for a splotch of red on the male bird's shoulder and *nowhere* else? Why should the common hen in her wild state, choose a noisy flaming colored mate who would invite trouble from birds and beasts of prey? Would that help them survive? As a matter of fact, the hen does not do the choosing. This theory was adopted to avoid the evidence of *design* in creation, which, they admitted would destroy their hypothesis. Putting the responsibility on the female or on survival of the fittest utterly fails when you inquire why there is evident design in the beauty of bird's eggs, mollusks and even in the leaves of the trees. Why should young birds bear beautiful markings not like either parent? Why should the worker bee which has no sex, be unlike either parent?

IT PUZZLED DARWIN.

If God did not plan that each kind of creature should have its own marks of identity in voice, color, shape, habits, instincts, tastes and handicap, then it is certain that sex selection or survival could not do it. Why

Arguments Against

Twenty-eight

should a rabbit make a track like the letter Y? What law would put rattles on a snake's tail? What pinch of necessity would give a turkey gobbler a whiplash on his nose, ugly meat beads on his neck and a paint brush on his breast? When the theorists explain the utility of the crowing of a rooster, they never tell you why he crows *at night*. Why is it that of all the kinds of creatures, no two kinds taste or smell alike?

RECKLESS WITH MILLIONS.

Evolutionists rely much on the study of fossils, and since it is out of reach of common people, poorly supported theories pass for facts. When this is written, the latest report on bones is published in the Scientific American, May, 1923. It says: "We must then trace our genealogy and that of the apes back 2,000,000 years before we come to a common meeting point." Speaking of bones, they say: "Those of the few discoveries of men and ape-like men more than 50,000 years old, could be placed in a handbag." They admit that some of these bones are in doubt. As a matter of fact, the bones may be those of an idiot, a freak, or a beast; or they may have been "planted" as a clever hoax, as some bones have turned out to be.

THE CONFESSION.

The first one dealt with is called "Pithecanthropus erectus" and might as properly be called "Evolvo-spoof-us," as they only

Twenty-nine

have the top of the skull. With one bone they have actually made a photograph of him from the waist up. More daring cartoonists have even made pictures of his tracks that pass for scientific. With only the top piece of the skull, they know that his nose was flat, that his chin was short and that he had a gentle eye and a bull neck. Of the "Heidelberg man," they have nothing but a jawbone. Because it is narrow, they decide that he could not speak a language, all of which proves that *a parrot cannot talk at all*. Even a goose-bone prophet would not presume so recklessly. Do you believe that with a hat full of bones (take this either way you wish) they can bridge the gulf of nearly two million years? Are you convinced that these supposed races were our ancestors? Then here is a cruel jolt. They say of four races represented by these bones, that they "LEFT NO DESCENDANTS."

CHILDLESS ANCESTORS."

After all the hullabaloo, after millions had accepted them as ancestors, it is now decided that they *left no descendants* and have passed out of existence without apparent reason. In their place we have Mutt and Jeff and Barney Google. Such artists as these, who can reconstruct a hypothetical race from an unidentified bone, would like to give your Bible a "scientific" tinkering. One of their drum majors says, "Everything has evolved,

Thirty

from molecule to Jehovah." "Man is not a fallen god, but a promoted reptile."

FISH GILLS FIFTY MILLION YEARS OLD.

Because there are three wrinkles on the head of the partly developed unborn child, they jump at the conclusion that they are "gill slits."* Against this presumption, I argue that they do not look like fish gills; they are not in the right place for gills; if our ancestors ever had gills, there is no reason why they should not have kept them for us; whatever may be the reason for these wrinkles, they are necessary to the development of the face of the child. It is a claptrap and flapdoodle philosophy, that will read into the fathomless mystery of unborn life, the markings of a fish, that they say lived fifty million years ago.

SEE FOR YOURSELF.

Another fairy tale is that our ancestors once squatted on a limb when it rained and held their hands over their heads as an umbrella. Now after two million years, they say the hair on the arms slants the way the water used to run. You may easily prove the folly of this, by observing that the hair on the forearm slants around the arm as though the ancestors drove an open automobile in the rain. The hair on the lower limbs would indicate that there were no floor boards and

---
*I have just read the statement of an eminent evolutionist that this nonsense is now abandoned.

Thirty-one

the splash of mud turned the hair towards the hips. Even so, it is better to be a fool in your right mind than to be a wise man drunk with infidel philosophy.

* * * *

UNDER FIRE.

A cerain gathering of pastors and laymen listened to the foregoing paper somewhat abridged and offered sharp criticism both in public and in private. Though three previous gatherings had applauded **eight** papers which presented the opposite views, the chief objection offered was that it is unwise to discuss these matters in public.

Those who know how the so-called modernist theories have been thrust, thinly disguised, into Sunday school literature and taught to lisping children, will need no answer. It is enough to say that if a defense of the unity and integrity of the Holy Scriptures, before Christians, will start a scrimmage, there is a confliflct long overdue.

Objection 2. If youthful minds are taught that faith is at variance with science, they will later accept science and abandon faith.

This has been answered repeatedly. We do not question the findings of science, but the fiat of alleged scientists. There is no possible chance that anyone can ever show that God did not make one man from the dust. If there were other beings like men; if God followed closely a pattern already found practical; if the human body was modified somewhat when "all flesh had corrupted his way"; if any one of several hypotheses are considered; then the evidence in man himself is on the side of Genesis. Whatever men guess, only God gives testimony concerning the first man in his image.

Objection 3. Most of the scholars have accepted the theory of evolution.

Many or few, the word accepted is well chosen. Not one in a thousand could take the witness stand and testify from personal observation and investigation. The veracity of the Scriptures is not to be impeached by counting noses or hearsay testimony. Of an event remote in time, never repeated and

Thirty-two

wholly beyond observation, a fool can give as competent testimony as a philosopher, since neither one was there. At the risk of seeming profane, I will say that scholarship has often been mistaken and is agreed now only on what is easily demonstrated. A free acting Omnipotent God has probably not kept within the limits they have set for him.

Objection 4. Who cares how we came, if we know where we are going?

As well might a gypsy fortune teller ask,—"Who cares how many lies I have told in the past, if I tell you what you wish to hear now?" There are but two possible sources of information concerning a life beyond the grave,—revelation and necromancy. If the revelation we incline to is sadly mixed with fable and fiction, the spirit medium will come into authority as the Bible hold upon the people is loosened, (and she has). If you are satisfied that science has discredited the Garden of Eden story, bear in mind, it has **not confirmed** life beyond the grave. "Begone miracle story! Hurrah for heaven!" is an idiotic slogan.

Objection 5. Why worry about critics? Let God take care of the Bible.

He will. Thus they taunted the dying Christ. When God answered, not one stone of the temple was left upon another. If aweless critics will read the handwriting of God in the dust of buried cities, they may surmise that the hand that wrote on Babylon's palace wall, may yet write for us.

Objection 6. You have failed utterly to discuss Christian evolution.

This is the tragedy; that a man called to be the prophet of God cannot see that in all the assumed billion years of evolution when it was helpful for the weak to go down before brute force and cunning, there was nothing that remotely resembled "the meekness and gentleness of Christ," who ministered to the poor and sick while he heaped woes upon the indifferent upper classes. Evolution is not Christianity; it is Nietzscheism. Nietzsche hated Christianity because it "glorified sympathy, tenderness, mercy, which are weaknesses and hindrances to power." If you can imagine moral deviltry and a heavenly hell then may we conceive of "Christian" evolution.

HOLINESS LIBRARY
EIGHT VOLUMES

Fletcher on Perfection $0.15
By John Fletcher.

A Plain Account of Christian Perfection. .... .15
By John Wesley.

Entire Sanctification .... .15
By Adam Clarke.

The Baptism With the Holy Ghost .. .. .15
By H. C. Morrison.

Scriptural Holiness .... .15
By B. A. Cundiff.

Sanctification, What it is, When it is, and How it is.. .15
By Collins.

The Second Work of Grace.. .15
What is it, Why have it, Scripturalness of it, How to Obtain it.
By C. W. Ruth.

The King's Gold Mine...... .10
Or The Conversion and Sanctification of the Disciples.
By Bud Robinson.

The above seven splendid titles need no comment as to what they contain, and their authors are so well known that they need no introduction. You can get them—about 400 pages—postpaid: One set 8 Vol., for $1.00.

Pentecostal Publishing Company,
Louisville, Ky.

Arguments Against

1ST EDITION   **20 CENTS**

PUDDLE TO PARADISE

BY B. H. SHADDUCK, PH.D.
AUTHOR OF
"JOCKO-HOMO HEAVENBOUND"

Arguments Against

PUDDLE TO PARADISE

By B. H. Shadduck, Ph.D.

"GREAT SWELLING WORDS"

The author does not allege that evoluters are the upper end of a fish-reptile-marsupial-lemur succession. They have classified him as ignorant because he has denied it; perhaps they will not be better pleased with this cartoon that ADMITS IT. The artist has tried to show the four kinds of tails that our ancestors (?) have had and lost and since the evolutionists insist that they were only a few months removed from "gill slits" when born, the cartoonist has conceded the "slits."

Copyright 1925 by B. H. Shadduck

Arguments Against

Two

JUST TO GET OUR BEARINGS

Many excuse me on the ground of ignorance.

If you will read with this impression, you will think for yourself instead of nursing theories left on your doorstep while you were overawed with scholarship.

No doctrine worth while is beyond the reach of the world's burden bearers—the common people. Only error needs to hide in a fog of words. My effort will be to translate the hocus-pocus of evolution into simple words, believing that the contradictions of this "science," if held up to the light, will not make much of a bluff.

In speaking of the Bible, I mean the Holy Scriptures accepted by Christ and the Apostolic Church.

If these pages are read by any POLITE person who has been unfortunate in the choice of ancestors, I regret that I must discuss the family's unhappy past. I would do anything to help you forget it.

I use the words "evoluter" and "evolution-ism" because they fit the man and the propaganda of the man who musses up his own ancestry with beasts that crawl and bark and gibber and then, to avoid shame, slanders the parentage of everyone else.

I FIGHT NOT ONE EVOLUTION, BUT TWO.

Evolution means survival by claw and fang and ambush and treachery. They have fixed up another goody-goody kind for the Sunday School. If they believe the brute kind was good TO GET US HERE, LET THEM PRACTICE WHAT THEY PREACH! EVOLUTION HAS NOT ONE LAW FOR FOUR LEGS AND ANOTHER FOR TWO.

The evoluter asks us to keep "hands off" his religion, while he destroys ours. Under the mask of "science," he vilifies our origin and mocks our faith in a miracle working God at the taxpayers' expense. He is willing to wink at some sort of hope-so heaven if we accept his frog-pond Eden.

If some wish to apologize for the Bible and adjust their faith to this loose-leaf creed, we do not want our children adjusted at our expense.

They are passing around a little phrase that is reckoned a withering retort. "I would as soon be made of an ape as a ball of mud." I sometimes wonder if they expect God himself to know what they mean if they don't know themselves. If they mean that God took the lime, carbon, water, etc., in an ape and made a man as a mill makes near silk of sawlogs, that is not evolution. It does not remotely approximate evolution. Evolution means that man was BORN of an ape and that there was no appreciable difference between the highest ape and the lowest man. They tell us that we yet retain some "hold-over" from every crawling worm or reptile our ancestors have ever been. All right, let's go.

Three

ONE LIMB BEARS HEAVEN FRUIT

"Jack and the Beanstalk" may have been a literary prophecy of the astounding story they ask us to believe. This tree is presumed to be 500,000,000 years old, more or less. There never was but the one tree and though there are countless billions of the same kind of seeds that this tree came from, ONLY ONE GREW AND NO OTHERS WILL SPROUT.

Four

IF EVOLUTION WORKED

Right now, I ought to have feathers on my arms. Pin feathers, anyhow.

As a boy, I longed for wings—soaring wings, flapping wings, bat-like wings, any kind of wings that would afford deliverance from plodding journeys.

According to the constitution and by-laws of evolution, I ought to have wings.

Do I talk like a fool?

No. I talk like a man who really thinks evolution will work right here and now—if there is one such.

One of the suppositions that go with the theory of evolution is that there was a time when the reptiles could not get where they were going, fast enough. (I have been in that fix myself.) Now another supposition is that when eyes were needed, "eyes came out to meet the need" and when ears were needed, they came out to hear. The reptiles needed wings; they needed them then and there, but when you want evolution to do anything, you must place your order a million years ahead. Evolution can't be hurried because that would be a miracle too miraculous. It seems that evolution looked the field over and selected a pair of reptiles with a long scale or hair or flap of skin on their legs and **mated them up.** (!) From the progeny, it chose a pair a wee bit more-so and **let them "survive."** Always selecting with **wings in mind,** its "survivors" became pretty birds and because it helped them survive, **they layed speckled eggs.**

If the Bible contained such folly, how evoluters would mock

The snakes that couldn't get feathers started did not die; **they ate birds. Evolution often feeds its "survivors" to those that have been** THEORETICALLY **survived.** I have been survived a great many times in the same way, because I didn't have wings.

You don't understand how a reptile could grow feathers?

Five

It isn't supposed to be understood. It has been spread out over such vast periods of time and the mystery has been so thinned out with gradual changes that it is supposed to soak through the cracks of your mind **without being understood.**

And yet, a feather is such a delicate, complicated, wonderful structure that one wonders how a feather machine could make itself, set itself up in the right place and push feathers out in exactly the right way. You see, if it got them wrong end to or wrong side out or didn't lap them just right, they would be only trouble makers. **You wonder just what a feather was, ten years before it was a feather.**

I don't know; ask the professor.

What I want to know is, what we have to do to get wings? Probably every normal minded barefooted boy since Cain and Abel hurt their feet with stones and briers, has wanted wings. Man has from the first been devising ways to get somewhere without walking. He has longed for wings so much that wings are in his poetry and associated with his heaven. Along with the want-to, there has been a dire need. Millions have lost their lives in times of danger, for want of wings. Surely we have met all the conditions. An eminent authority (McCook) says a "17 year locust" (Cicada) grows wings from "buds" in 15 minutes. How do we proceed to get "buds"?

Evolute is an imaginary verb in the past tense. The farther back in the past you assume its magic, the more the mystery fades and the more "scientific" it becomes. Imagine a professor saying to his class, "This frog is beginning to get ready to develop wings," or "This toad has started to commence to develop a marsupial pouch," or "I see in this turtle a drift that indicates turtles will some day nurse their young."

Some theories must not be pushed too far.

And yet, evolution is a very convincing theory if you wish to believe it and need it as a poultice for

Six

sin. Jesus said false prophets would arise with an amazing show of seeming proof. (Matt. 24:24) Did he mean evoluters? Well, *it is certain he did not mean people who believe the Bible* TOO MUCH. His warning ought to make his people cautious. There is always a contradiction in false doctrine.

THE TALE OF A PAIL

My neighbor tells a pig story in four chapters.

(1) He bought a half starved runt of a pig. (2) He fed it a bucket of slop and it squealed for more. (3) He fed it a second bucket of slop and it asked for more. (4) He put the pig in the bucket and the bucket was not nearly full.

I can believe either end of the story by itself.

My neighbor seems to believe all of it because when he tells one part he isn't thinking of the other parts.

It is easy to give mental assent to conflicting ideas, if you keep them so far apart that they do not bump each other. All I ask of students of evolution is to bring its contrary theories into focus at the same time.

There are some sincere souls who think they believe in the Bible and evolution and *the more they believe in one, the less they believe in the other.* Others think they have effected a working compromise, but the compromise is usually all on one side. I want no harmony that will back the Bible in on a switch to let the circus train go by. I want to bring on a head end collision—in your minds at least. I am not unmindful of those students who would like to believe the Bible, but have had evolution-ism dinned into them till their minds follow the beaten path. If such students will try to undo the dinning long enough to consider all that is *missing, misapplied or contradictory* in the testimony, I have no fears for the Bible. If you have reached the place where you look for contradictions in the Bible and connected truth in

Seven

THE MODERN MISUSE OF THE BIBLE

There are three types of flaw-picking critics of the Bible.

(1) The Bible is fallible; I am not! Let me guide you.

(2) The Bible is fallible; so am I! Let me guide you.

(3) The Bible is fallible or I am! Let me guide you.

If you know any Bible rival who claims some other classification, let me know.

Wonderful self reliance! A man who admits that his brain is less than SIX INCHES FROM HIS GILL SLITS appoints himself a censor of the Eternal Word. What will they not do when they evolve once more?

Eight

evolution, isn't it time to reverse the process in the interest of fair play?

CIRCUMSTANTIAL EVIDENCE

It is obvious that the only possible evidence of what happened when man appeared on earth must be circumstantial, *unless the only eye witness is permitted to testify.* If what purports to be God's testimony is received, it is against evolution.

I am well aware that many attempts have been made to turn this testimony into "allegory" and make it fit evolution, but allegory must not be made to mean exactly the opposite of what it says. Here is a summary of the testimony and the "allegory."

THE BIBLE

God formed man of the dust.
God breathed into his nostrils and he became a living soul.
This was to fulfil the plan to make man in God's image.
In the catalog of animals, there was not one fit to be his mate.
Adam was put into deep sleep and a mate made from a rib.
They were warned not to do a certain thing.
A **reinterpreter** appeared and persuaded Eve that God did not mean exactly what he said and promised an evolution to something better.
Man fell and the curses followed.

THE "ALLEGORY"

God made man by proxy; an ape mammy furnished the "dust."
He took a breath for himself when he was born, **like other apes.**
He was not made in God's image; just started to evolve in that direction.
His mate was another ape product; the ape acting for God, of course.
Man fell slowly, painfully UP.
The other details are "folk lore."

Why this labored effort?

Evidently to thin out the miracle of creation so that anti-miracle "christians"

Nine

with weak stomachs can take a little broth. To borrow a phrase from electricians, unbelievers want their miracles "stepped down" to a very low **voltage**. When you begin making allegories out of miracles, there is no logical stopping place till you make an allegory of God. If we knew the details of Adam's physical make-up before the fall and knew that he had neighbors made on much the same physical pattern, was there anyone to forbid God making him just that way as a specal creative act?

Let us illustrate with another miracle. Exodus 4 records the story of a stick that God turned into a snake. Can you say with a certainty on which you would risk your soul, "God couldn't do it; if it was like a snake, it was born of a snake that evolved from a fish"?

Is the New Testament allegory also? Matt. 3:9 says, "God is able of these stones to raise up children unto Abraham." If God did just that thing they might resemble men without having any evolutionary connection with man or monkey. If creation is impossible in Genesis, it is impossible in Matthew.

Surely there *cannot be any possible evidence* that a God who did make a serpent from a stick and could make a man from a stone, could not have made his image man immediately and like anything else he pleased.

Evolution-ism, when you simmer it down, puts ape limitations on man and human limitations on God. They assume that we are only a pint of brains ahead of an ape, and as for God—he must have been limited to what man's brain approves.

Some will concede that *God could do it*, but they shrink from *overworking* him. Some will say, "Must we believe the improbable?"

Is creation improbable?

Arguments Against

Ten

If it is, evolution is impossible. How else could there be the first life for evolution to start with?

To say that it started itself, is disastrous, for there would be ***no one to stop it, if there was no one to start it.*** It is just as necessary to the theory of evolution to stop the process that would produce the first life as to start it. If it could start one place at one time, it could start in many places, many times. ***If you leave the gate open like that,*** 30 minutes of time and a ten-acre swamp would generate enough "ancestors" to give each form of life a little forefather of its own.

Is that clear?

It is vital to the theory of ***one ancestor for all,*** to presume a some-how-or-other starter to start one little lone progenitor, and have another presumption to stop the starter ***before it starts two.*** Otherwise there might be a different origin for each kind of creature, and that would be CREATION ***thinned out by a process.*** That would permit each kind to be brought forth "after their kind." This could not explain the creation of Adam, but it would ruin the theory of evolution utterly.

DONATIONS

No man has ever been able to string together the guesses of evolutionism and make a theory, without donating the string. It requires mental contributions to fill up the gaps. When the first life appeared, ***it could have nothing by inheritance.*** It was an ORPHAN before it happened. It was blind, deaf, brainless and invisible, if it had any internal "laws," or instinct, you must donate them. You must donate the presumption that some presiding ***substitute-for-a-miracle,*** gave it a chemical laboratory, factories and machines to transmit to others, to make feathers, hair, wool, bone, fins, fiddles and all the balance of equipment known to life. Every thing that has ever come out of that life ***must have been in it then or has***

Eleven

been donated since. You must donate *chance* to get such freaks as the fish that carries a light on the end of a pole. You must donate *luck* to prevent some one form evolving a destroyer that would put an end to all the others. Suppose some insect that works havoc now, had grown as large as an elephant?

The controversy really hangs on the question, Could God make man just as the Book says he did? If you say, "No," it shows what this 'ism leads to. If you say, "Yes, but I don't think he did," it is then a matter of theory and *theory is not science.*

ONLY THEORIES

For every theory of evolution, there is a theory of creation, just as reasonable, which would nullify it. I suggest a few, but remember they are only theories. I have no wish to inflict another supplement to the Bible, on a world already cursed with man-made revelation. *Faith is only a plaything* if it cannot outlast a California redwood, but must be rebuilt for every crop of toadstools.

(1) Many able expositors believe the second verse of the Bible describes the wreck of a world formerly inhabited. Continents may have blown up and gone down, leaving the sky black with smoke and gas. If this be true ancient fossils have no value as evidence.

(2) There may have been man-like animals before Adam and during his life. Some creature called "nachash" in the Hebrew, "was more subtle than any beast of the field." It seems not to have surprised Eve that he should talk and claim to know as much about religion as God did. He convinced her that his plans were evolutionary and would evolve her to a "higher" state. If you think of him as a serpent, remember, the serpent shape was later.

(3) Genesis 6 records the story of cross breeding that corrupted the race. "The Nephilim were in the earth in those days and also after that . . ." There

Twelve

are three interpretations of this obscure passage, none of them wholly convincing, but it is clear that there was a mix-up that greatly displeased God. After the flood there was another appearance of Nephilim, recorded in Num. 13:33. If they ever find a skull of the Nephilim, how they will cavort.

(4) God remade the nachash; introduced thorns and thistles, marked Cain, reduced the age of man twice, gave beast heart and habits to Nebuchadnezzar, prepared a fish for Jonah, and there is nothing in the Bible to say he may not have made many other changes in animals and men. Since man has worshipped beasts, sinned with beasts and thought like beasts, there may have been a "mark of the beast" long before the one spoken of in Revelation. Certainly we are not now as God made man.

(5) There is much that we do not know about prenatal markings called "birth marks." We do not know how much the mind may affect the body or what changes sin may have worked in past centuries.

(6) The Bible teaches that God has, at times, accommodated those who "did not like to retain God in their KNOWLEDGE." (Rom. 1:23,28) **The man who prefers brute ancestry ought to be humored enough to let him believe he has.** I do not say that 2 Thes. 2:11 refers to such men, but I will say it cannot refer to eager believers in the words of him who said, "If ye believed Moses, ye would believe me." God may have had arrogant scholarship in mind when he made all creatures.

(7) According to the showing of evolution-ists, there are more forms "degenerate" among visible creatures, than there are forms maintaining their place. Then why not presume that bones that indicate half-way stages (if any do) are from degenerate creatures that have gone back rather than forward? This would fit the teachings of the Book.

Not only can we nullify evolutionary theories with

Thirteen

other theories, but *their theories nullify themselves.*

THEORIES THAT KILL THEMSELVES

Someone has thought up a slogan, "Facts Are Final," and the children of the "mud puppy" (or whatever it was) wonder why the children of the rib-woman do not surrender. The pity is that the student mistakes theories for facts. There are only three general facts, all of which, if not overworked or padded, *are in accord with the Bible.* Here they are:

(a) Certain forms of life are similar to other forms.

(b) Certain forms appeared before other forms.

(c) Certain forms are not just what they were long ago.

We need not discuss these facts except as we discuss the *theories of how they came to be facts.* I expect to show that evolutionary theories cannot explain the facts because its theories are contradictory.

DIRIGIBLE EVOLUTION

If facts are final, when did evolution-ism reach any finality?

A friend of mine who is an eminent college president, has sent me a learned treatise, to set me right. The important words in the title are the "TREND of Evolution."

What a fitting name!

For the benefit of child readers, let me explain that "trend" means it is leaving the place where it is and going to some place where it isn't. Just like sheep in short pasture. Ever since I can remember, they have been *trending.*

THE LAW OF EVOLUTIONARY LAWYERS

There are certain laws of life, well known to stock breeders, that the prophets of the bog, by fog or pettifog, harness to their 'ism. Put in simple language,

Fourteen

these are, VARIATION, HEREDITY, ADJUSTMENT, SELECTION.

VARIATION

Variation is the law that no two, born of the same parents, are alike. Adam must have known that, but how can it unroll, unwind or evolve *a machine where there isn't one?* The stockman takes advantage of variation, but he does what the law cannot do for itself. To develop a characteristic, he line-breeds the freaks to develop the freakishness. Arbitrary selection, segregation and line-breeding will produce a herd of Holsteins on one side of a fence and Jerseys on the other. Never in a million years will Nature, left to itself to go haphazard, do that. Nature will do exactly the opposte and *left to itself will breed to a common level. Nature resists the breeder* and if the fence is broken down for two years it will upset the work of fifty years.

Question for the class in mathematics:

If nature, left to itself, will in two years upset the work of fifty years, how long will it take nature to do all the breeder can do and work a miracle that he wouldn't believe if he saw it? How long would it take to evolve a hog into something else that does not look like a hog, taste like a hog, smell like a hog, act like a hog, and give it an equipment that hogs do not need and *it cannot do without*?

When the breeder has done his most and his best, cows are only cattle and hogs continue to be swine. He can't turn them into camels or coyotes. Nature when it has done its most and its best (left to itself) will make scrubs out of thoroughbreds. All the breeder can do is to MODIFY THE STRUCTURES THE ANIMAL ALREADY HAS. The stockman can breed a white belt around a black hog, but he can't breed antlers on to its head. To grow a hair or a horn or a feather requires a machine in the body that can man-

Fifteen

ufacture just that. Evolution undertakes to unwrap in a creature, what that form of life never had.

Man is having trouble with his teeth; will the "scientists" kindly tell us how we may unroll or evolve a gizzard?

Much is made of the fact that breeders can breed certain equipment off. That is not evolution, *it is the opposite.* One of the eminent "authorities" on evolution says there are 180 structures in the human body that we have lost the use of, wholly or in part, *because we ceased to use them.* They say all mammals are in much the same fix.

Please underscore that with red ink. We will need it later.

THAT CONFESSION OUGHT TO SINK THE SYSTEM FOREVER.

Is evolution a process of subtraction?

Unless they can show that we have 180 structures getting ready to be used, MAN IS HEADED THE WRONG WAY. If losing the use of ourselves is evolution, then death must be a grand evolutionary spurt. One hundred and eighty disappearing structures are 180 arguments against evolution and 180 arguments that only the grace of God can keep man from the junk pile. "Except ye repent," ye shall lose all the rest of yourself.

Millions and millions of creatures, ALL GOING, NONE COMING. They do not tell us of one organ that we are going to have. If they could find one tail feather on a frog, they would have one argument for evolution. Why don't they graft one on just to make a showing? They are already borrowing grafts from the monkeys to restore OVER-EVOLVED men; here's hoping they graft brains next.

If an unused organ must recede, then the evolution of a new organ would be a-b-s-o-l-u-t-e-l-y impossible, because an organ can't be used before we get it and while we are getting it before it can be used, it MUST RECEDE.

Arguments Against

Sixteen

They say that apes can wiggle their ears and most men cannot. This, they argue, is evidence that when men ceased to be apes, they began to lose that CON-VENIENCE along with other advantages. If we could and the apes could not, *that would also prove evolution.* Whether the wiggle is coming or going, "ALL IS GRIST THAT COMES TO THE EVO-LUTER'S MILL." Elephants can wiggle their noses more than we can; that proves we evolved from elephants.

RACHET WHEEL HEREDITY

Heredity is the stubborn law of life that would fight evoluton to the last ditch. Evolution-ism must have a docile heredity that will listen to reason. It can only use heredity that will *loosen up* long enough to get a change of equipment and then *tighten up* long enough to fix the change. It must be like a rachet wheel; let evolution go forward and catch it when it tries to fly back. This made-to-order heredity has allowed our ancestors to lose four kinds of tails, but insists on fish gills in the unborn.

ADJUSTMENT, NOT INVENTION

God has planted in all life an ability to adjust itself to changed conditions and environment, *within limits.* The Bible does not guarantee fixity of type such as the length of a bone or the color of a feather. It does guarantee a fixity of what it calls "kind" so that nature can never turn a turkey into a goose. Move a polecat to a cold climate and it will grow heavier fur and not take a geological *age to do it.* Move it to a rainy climate and it will not grow an umbrella in any period of time. Nature may modify what the creature has, but *cannot create an organ that it has not.* The boy who persists in smoking will find his body speedily adjusts itself to nicotine, so that nausea ceases, and it does not take glaciers, sinking con-

Seventeen

tinents and earthquakes to do it; but he will not grow a pipe or smokestack while the world standeth.

One eminent writer explains that deer developed antlers because for ages, the males pushed their heads together and made callous places that finally turned into horns.

If pressure will produce horns, why have they not developed on man's feet?

Why does the deer shed his antlers?

Why should he have more spikes on his antlers each year?

Why should horns grow in forks with one animal and spirals with another?

Isn't it about time for work horses to get the beginnings of horns on their shoulders?

If bruises produce horns, the turtle and porcupine must have had some activity like football.

Some exponents of the doctrine have abandoned this theory. In fact, there is no phase of evolution that someone has not abandoned.

Not only are creatures unable to develop what they have not got, but what they haven't got does not need to be developed. If a creature can get along without a marsupial pouch to carry its babies in (AND THEY DO), what is the distressing need that will evolve one? Whatever handicap the creatures have, they hold their own. The slow going toad catches insects *enough* and that is all a swallow can do. Not being able to go South, the toad doesn't need to. The bat with its wings, has not crowded out the mouse that must go afoot.

"SURVIVAL OF THE FITTEST"

The "survival of the fittest" has fooled millions. It is as convincing as a cast iron lion in the dark.

Here is a little question for the professor.

WHEN THE FITTEST SURVIVE AND THE LESS FIT OUTLIVE THEM, WHICH IS THE "SURVIVINGEST" SURVIVOR?

Arguments Against

Eighteen

According to the program, the creature fartherest back in the surviving process is the amoeba. It has been "survived" more than any other form of life on earth, (if this survival law is not foolishness) yet it keeps right on living though numberless "survivors" have become extinct. Its numbers are *limited only by infinity.*

The entire fabric of evolution depends on the false theory that what they call *"higher" and "later" forms of life, are better fitted to survive.* It takes for granted a presumption that life has evolved for hundreds of millions of years from amoeba to man because each "higher" form was better able to survive than the one beneath it.

What spoils this "bedtime story" is the fact that stubborn "lower" forms persist where the "higher" forms cannot. Is it the truth or a lie, that numberless billions of one celled creatures can be dried up, frozen up, buried in the mud or blown away and come right back and do business?

Ask any school boy who has studied biology.

Of course there is an element of truth in this survival theory. Old mammy toad will leave a thousand eggs in a pool. Averages indicate that only one can live to the second year. Now it is obvious that if one little tadpole can outwit *all* the foes and get *all* the food when there is only enough for one, he has quite the best chance to make his mother a grandma.

But, the spryest little fellow may be the one first within reach of a foe. The most cautious one may be the one that goes without its dinner. With death lurking on four sides, above and below, I will pick the average tadpole for the winner. If they were more helpless or stupid a million years ago, it is difficult to understand how any of them lived.

No doubt if black and white rabbits were turned loose to run wild, they would, in time, breed back to a common color that was protective, and that is about

Nineteen

all that "survival" can do for them. Some student will say, "Surely, the fastest rabbits will survive and raise the average of speed." This seems plausible until you consider that their natural foes use strategy and stealth as much as speed. Speed in a rabbit begets over confidence and does damage when it makes short turns in the briers.

Now suppose this survival theory could add speed, size and sagacity, that would not be evolution because the rabbit would still be a rabbit. If "survival" could give the rabbit an equipment like a skunk, that would be evolution for the rabbit, but it would be EVIL-ution for everything else. Imagine, if you can, how soon other life would be driven out. Now evolution has had millions of years (they say) and millions of chances to develop in some creature an equipment that would destroy competitors, but each form of life has **enough** equipment and **not too much**. It would take a board of scientists a thousand years to figure out so nice a balance as we see in nature. Would evolution do that?

It is a vital part of the law of "survival" that no creature can develop an equipment that hinders it or helps its foes.

Is that true, professor?

If the so called "higher" forms of life are so handicapped in the struggle for food and mates and progeny and against fire, frost, famine, flood and foes that "lower" forms are not quickly driven out, then it argues that they were created that way. Never mind what some propagandist says about it; use your common sense. You can see that one bird lays but one egg, another 16. One animal is short on speed, another on wit, another on defense, another on the variety it can eat, another on progeny, so that a wonderful balance is preserved. (Job 39:17.)

I quite agree with evolution-ism that water life appeared first. The Bible says so. We believe it pleased

Arguments Against

Twenty

God to create life in the order he did. The evolution-ist *must begin as near nothing as possible so that it will minimize the miracle of getting the first life and not overwork the necessity of creation.* Having presumed one invisible life, the next thing to presume is that through all the ages nature put a premium on the more complicated forms and gave a bonus of life and progeny to those that developed brain, speed, defense, etc.

That is exactly what evolution would do if evolution were a fact.

THAT IS EXACTLY WHAT HAS NOT BEEN DONE BECAUSE IT IS NOT A FACT.

Every advantage has some corresponding handicap, disproving evolution.

On this proposition, I am willing to stake the fight.

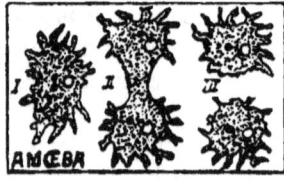

Let us begin at the beginning.

Here is a greatly magnified picture of the little bag of soup that they say started the trouble. The first figure shows the little ancestor getting ready to have a puckering in its equator. Figure 2 shows the furniture divided and moved, half in each end. Fig. 3 shows it broken in two **without hurting it.** How it could know when to move the furniture or how to move it or where to move it, when it has no brains or nerves, we do not know. Since there must be heredity, variation and survival to get evolution started, will the professor kindly advise us which end gets the heredity and which end survived? Since each end is the other end of the other end, how are we to get variation started? Since the ones that live now are presumed to be divisions of the first one and stubbornly refuse to evolve, it is difficult to see how any variation could help them.

Twenty-One

Why should a creature that can multiply by division and add to its numbers by subtraction, adopt a sex complication that would double the hazard, slow up the process, start a fight among rivals and cumber the settlement with more or less helpless infancy?

Would sex help sexless creatures to resist calamity?

Suppose, just to be generous, we donate sex to evolution, (I don't know any other way it could get it) so that it can get heredity, variation and **plenty of fights started.**

Now why should a creature that can lay from a hundred to ten million eggs that will *hatch themselves*, forsake that prolific, care-free method and lay only a few eggs that must be kept warm?

After laying eggs for a hundred million years or so, why should any creature junk the equipment and install the more troublesome system of birth?

Why should creatures that could produce young that could take care of themselves, add to their troubles and help their foes by producing young that needed to be hovered, guarded and fed?

Perhaps some clever theorist can juggle words and make you believe that the more helpless the young creatures are and the fewer they are, the more there will be of them.

Why should creatures that are equally at home in the water or on land, able to get food or seek safety in either place, limit themselves to the land? Is there any such creature now that could utterly forsake the water and flourish?

Why should creatures having cold blood, requiring comparatively little food, suffering no harm when they freeze solid, adopt hot blood, so they suffer from cold and need more food? Why should any creature work an injury to itself, if evolution is supervising the job?

There is only one answer to these questions. The

Twenty-Two

Personal Creator who maintains a balance of life on earth, *hangs handicaps on those creatures, that because of superior equipment in other ways, might banish other life.*

I do not know what God's plan for the creatures was before "all flesh had corrupted their way upon the earth"; (Gen. 6:12) (See Is. 11:7.) I only remind you that life as it is, has a distribution of advantage, handicap and hazard *utterly foreign to any blind haphazard drift of evolution.*

It must be apparent to all that to prolong the period of helpless infancy, is to multiply the hazard of death before maturity. If evolution has done that, it has *made lies out of its own laws.* They have tried to escape this by presuming that a prolonged helplessness in infancy insures a longer mature life, but this is not true. The 17 year "locust" has 17 years' infancy and a few days of adult life. The turtle, goose, and many other creatures are helpless for only a brief period, yet they live to great age.

There is also a handicap in being "educated" past the place where you can believe God and see simple facts.

If an evoluter could visit Mars and find the order of life *exactly opposite,* so that life seemed to flow from the complex to the simple, he would come back and say, "They have evolution up there also."

DOUBLE BARRELED EVOLUTION

If evolution is true it is a combination like a tin can connected to a dog at the tail. Each end keeps the other busy.

It takes a sexless creature and develops in it a need for a mate at the same time it is developing a mate that needs to be needed.

How thoughtful! What rare foresight!

It takes a creature with cold blood, gives it hot

Twenty-Three

blood so it can freeze to death and makes it a fur coat so it will not. It takes eggs that will hatch themselves and makes them need to be hovered and changes the mother's mind so she is obsessed with a desire to hover them. It takes swamp babies able to hustle for themselves and makes them need warm milk at exactly the same time that it fixes up a mother that needs to be milked.

It is as wonderful as a blind paper hanger matching all the figures as he works, by the smell of the flowers on the paper, but you must believe it or be called ignorant.

A WHALE OF A TALE OF THE TAIL OF A WHALE

They say the whale was a fish many million years ago, with a tail like other fish, and it could lay thousands of eggs in the sand and dismiss the matter. Most fish are content to stay in the water, but the fishy ancestors of the whale had evolution in them and took spells of wandering about on the land. Because it helped them survive, they lost their fish tail and got another kind. You see, change of habits and shape helped them survive and surviving helped them to change their habits and shape.

Very convenient arrangement!

After a million years or so, these once-upon-a-time fish were not fish any more. They were Mytholizards or something just as needless. They ought to have been content with this, but they had evolution in them and in order to survive, they had to unroll again and this time they turned into Fabricated-Hyperboles or something just as uncertain. By this time they could no longer lay a case of eggs but had only one lone baby that needed warm milk. There are only a few people who know the particulars of what happened next, but as nearly as I can find out, there was a shortage of phosphorus or protein in the diet and two of these Hypothetical-Metaphors GOT AWAY FROM EVOLUTION and went right back to the sea to live very happy as backsliders. Of course they needed a fish tail again and evolution forgave the runaways and gave them a fish tail again in the place where their other tail had been, but somehow the thing slipped and the new fish tail was **put on wrong** so that it extends East and West instead of North and South.

There is a sad chapter left out of the story by the explainers.

All the millions of its kind that did not go back to the sea, DIED.

Twenty-Four

Every kind of brute their ancestors ever had been, DIED.

Not one intermediate form left; only the quitters lived. After evolution had worked for millions of years to get their ancestors out of the water *so they could survive*, then to go back to the water and survive, when the ones that stayed with evolution all died; that makes it embarrassing for the explainers. They might write a book entitled "Why Whales Leave Home." As it is, they call the whale an "aberrant form" or a "degenerate."

BACKSLIDERS

The whale is the biggest backslider for which they offer apology, but by no means an isolated case. Common people who have heard only the *evolution side of evolution*, will be surprised to learn that of creatures big enough to be seen, *most of them are classed as* "DEGENERATES." (!)

They don't like me to tell this.

Nearly all parasites, as lice, ticks, mites, scale, and the multitude of internal "boarders" are classified by evolutionists as "degenerate." By "degenerate," they mean they have left some "higher" level. There are three well known parasites that live on a hen and many more trouble-makers inside. Even fish have lice and other parasites. Some parasites have parasites.

This is a good place to stop and think.

If evolution has done anything, the most of its work has been to make "degenerates."

I don't blame the little one celled fellows for refusing to go on a pilgrimage. Do you?

Now when you tabulate the results of evolution according to their own claims, this is what you get.

(1) Most of the living creatures remain one-cell.
(2) Transitional forms are nearly all dead.
(3) Many of the "higher" forms ended in extinction.
(4) Of those that went with evolution and escaped extinction, most of them are degenerate.
(5) The forms from which the "degenerates" degenerated are all dead.

Twenty-Five

(6) All mammal forms are losing some of their structures.
(7) Man, the shining example of what evolution can do, is losing 180 structures and getting no new ones in their stead.

After such a showing, they would like to commence on the Bible.

SEX SELECTION

Evoluters are a little shy about this "sex selection" process. Many of them have abandoned it. We could forgive them if they would admit that, the facts they cannot use, weigh on the side of creation.

The theory presumes that birds and bugs and butterflies have color marks and designs because, for millions of years, the females selected for mates those suitors that came nearest to their IDEAL.

It sounds as convincing as a college yell.

WHERE WOULD THE LADY BIRD OR BUG OR BUTTERFLY GET THE IDEAL?

If you can imagine these creatures getting an exquisite taste from nowhere, how could it happen that all the birds or bugs or butterflies of a kind, would AGREE on exactly the same colors in the same place of the same design and stick to it for a million years?

Of all creatures, women have the best taste, yet if seven women were made a committee to select a design for an ideal man, in the end, they would submit seven designs. Yet we are asked to believe that all the females of any particular species agreed exactly on a design and refused to have mates that did not *try* to meet the plans and specifications.

How would that explain the markings of young birds (when different from parents) or caterpillars that are wholly different from papa and mamma or the golden trimmings of the pupa? How would it explain the marvelous beauty of creatures that are blind, as revealed or amplified by the microscope?

These questions might be multiplied and made to include the song of birds and the bray of donkeys, but what is the use? The stubborn facts are that most

Twenty-Six

matings are determined by combat or happen-so. Common sense must be away on a vacation, if a man who knows ducks and their fondness for mud, can believe that mammy duck is concerned about the curl on the tail of her drake.

SIMILARITY IN ANATOMY

The fact that man is much like some animals in physical structure, is urged as a proof that he must have descended from the same ancestor. This argument is absolutely unanswerable, if you are sure that God could not use the same general pattern in making creatures to meet the same physical environment, and you are sure that man has not changed since he first appeared. Are you sure? (Is. 55:9.)

Man has four limbs; so has an ape. What of it? Must God have a different BEST for every creature? I am willing to surrender right now, if someone who knows how God could not do as he thinks he did, will come forward and tell us how God could have made millions of forms and had them all so different that men with highly evolved brains would accept his statement of creation.

Vernon Kellogg (evolutionist), in describing "undoubtedly the lowest of all mammal forms," tells of certain animals that "deposit a single egg in an external pouch, and there it hatches." Why call it the "lowest form"? If life began in the amoeba for all of us, then evolution has had just as long to work on the pedigree of this beast as on mine. In what way have the animals that went higher gained any advantage? According to the contradictory program of evolution-ism, the "earlier" and "lower" forms of life laid anywhere from a hundred to ten million eggs, and as life went "UP" the ladder there were fewer and fewer babies. According to program, this one-egg mammal must be *next to the very top*. Evolution can go no higher than to take its favorites to where they refuse to have any babies.

Twenty-Seven

How did this creature come to limit itself to one? Would that help the family survive? How did it originate that egg pocket? If it happened in one generation, it was CREATION. If it took many generations, then it developed while it could not be used and this is neither in accord with evolution nor with nature as we know it.

Did the animal evolve a pocket incubator by trying for a thousand generations to find a place to put its egg, or did it hit upon the plan of laying an egg because it had a pocket with nothing to put in it? Perhaps it held the egg up against the place where a pocket was desired till the pocket "came out to meet the need."

If you believe this, you can qualify as a "Mother Goose" enthusiast.

If this creature is an ancient "transitional form," a kind of station where the creatures change cars, why did the "higher" creatures get rid of this portable hatchery? Isn't it the handiest baby arrangement on earth? Do evoluters predict that other "lower" forms will get this arrangement before they use it and lose it while they are using it?

PERFECT BALANCE

There must be a BEST plan for God to follow in making a creature to fit particular habits, purposes, climates, foods, and resist foes. Now it follows that God must make some other creature that meets nearly the same conditions, on nearly the same pattern, if he does his best. The variation in equipment must keep up with the variation in conditions and the advantages and handicaps must preserve a balance, no more, no less than enough to keep one from driving others out.

BEAUTY AND ODDITY

In addition to variation for the sake of balance, God has added beauty and oddity. If his sole purpose

Twenty-Eight

in doing this was to disprove evolution, **he has done it well.** Evolution will be a long time explaining the "identification" marks and manners of all life.

WHAT SIMILARITY PROVES

Meat platters, soup plates, dinner plates, pie plates and saucers have a similarity. Now suppose we dig in the pottery yard and find broken saucers below broken meat platters, does that prove that they fed saucers into one end of a machine and took platters out at the other end? Is the little dish a many-times-grandmother to the big one? Have the cream pitcher and sugar bowl descended from a marble? On the contrary, it indicates that one maker made each one for a different purpose—*of the same clay.* It is hardly consistent for our evolvo tutors to insist that an amoeba would make us alike and a God could not.

EVOLUTION BY FITS AND STARTS

If all forms of life have developed from the amoeba, there ought to be a *continuous upward flow, showing creatures in every stage of evolution getting ready to be what they are not.* If there are forms a million years apart, why not a thousand or a hundred years apart? To avoid this fair inference, they say the intermediate forms are extinct. Who killed them and forbade others coming on? As a matter of fact, there is not one living creature between amoeba and man that they are sure is the form through which our evolution passed. They can only agree that our ancestors were *some sort* of marsupials, reptiles, amphibians, fish, etc. Unless evolution goes by jerks, there ought to be SOMETHING A LITTLE MORE AND SOMETHING A LITTLE LESS THAN EVERY FORM WE HAVE AND THE STREAM OUGHT TO KEEP COMING. In order to bridge the mighty chasm between man and reptiles, they assume that our distant ancestors were something like a kangaroo or opossum. Why are there no creatures

Twenty-Nine

10 per cent, 20 per cent and 30 per cent more than opossum and less than opossum? Where evidence is most needed, it is always missing. They are very free to tell you what the animals and birds **have been**, but are quite too shy and modest to tell you what any animal **will become**.

If humming birds and eagles have evolved from reptiles, then there ought to be some forms 99 per cent reptile and one per cent bird, others 98-2 per cent, 97-3 per cent, on up to 1 per cent reptile and 99 per cent bird. Among all the reptiles, will some expert pick out any kind of reptile that will turn into any kind of bird? If anyone will undertake the job, I will gladly print his forecast in the next edition.

It is necessary to assume that evolution has gone forward in waves killing off all between the waves, ending some waves in total extinction, letting most of the waves degenerate, and now the waves have stopped coming and man is losing 180 conveniences he formerly had.

THEY ASSUME A GULF OF HUNDREDS OF MILLIONS OF YEARS AND BRIDGE IT WITH OBITUARIES.

Why must they assume so much?

I think I know.

It is for the same reason that when a beautiful heiress gets shipwrecked, she selects a tropical island where a wonderful young hero has been marooned by cruel plotters. It enables him to rescue her from sharks while the sailors all drown. It affords them a chance to kill savages and wild beasts and discover a gold mine and be rescued soon after her wicked uncle dies. How else could they marry at $1.50 per copy?

BONES AND STONES

To support the assumption that connecting links are extinct, they appeal to fossils. In this field they have a double advantage. (a) Not one in a hundred is

Arguments Against

Thirty

able to examine the evidence, much less understand it. (b) Once they find a bone, they can name it what they please, date it when they please, add as much ink or plaster of paris as they please, and who can hinder them? Newspapers are ready to feature any guess or any picture they care to fabricate.

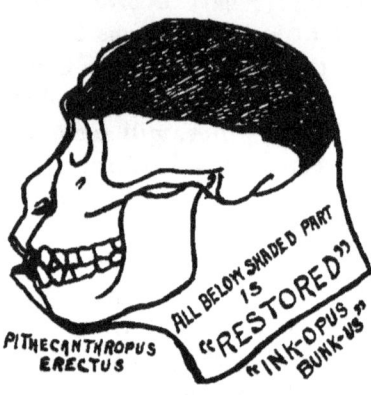

PITHECANTHROPUS ERECTUS

Here are two samples of how it is done. The Pithecanthropus Erectus is the name of a bone and what ink goes with it. (If you can't pronounce it, it m u s t be scientific.) The shaded portion represents a piece of skull bone. The outline shows how they think the former owner **ought to have looked to fit their theory.** To know that a bone had a flat nose and wore a No. 24 collar, is SUPERscience. It apes divinity. They make no report as to whether the gentleman had freckles. Perhaps they do not know.

On the following page is another job of "restoring." Two bones and two teeth are called "The Sussex Man." It is adapted and drawn to scale from a magazine article entitled "SCIENCE." The face and head are how he "might have looked." If you will cut out a piece of paper exactly like the bones and lay it over the savage face, you will see that to make the "Sussex man" fit the theory of evolution, his head is made too small for the skull bone and his face much too long for the jaw bone.

You can feed this sort of "science" to anyone who is as willing and trusting as a young robin when he gets his dinner.

So far as is certainly known, life appeared on earth

Thirty-One

"THE SUSSEX MAN" alias The FLIM FLAMUS
(By Courtesy of Hearst's Magazine.)

in substantially the order that is given in Genesis. All the experts seem to agree that there are great gaps in the records of the rocks and that so far as these records go, some forms appeared abruptly. If there were intermediate forms, they have been lost in the gaps. Many of the claims of great geologists and paleontologists are disputed by others equally great.

Thirty-Two

The author is not competent to pass upon these claims. We may all of us use common sense and to such it will be apparent that to prove one animal lived before another, does not prove one descended from the other. If the bones of a Shetland pony are found beneath the bones of a draft horse, there is yet room for doubt that the Shetland was the ancestor. No matter where you find the bones, the lap dog is not the father of the Great Dane.

If someone digs us out 10,000 years hence, they may find tomato cans under automobiles. They may show that tomato cans preceded automobiles. Even if they prove that no nation ever produced automobiles till after eating tomatoes, it will not prove that tomatoes caused automobiles, much less that automobiles evolved from cans, with an intermediate wheelbarrow missing.

In order to disprove creation, the rocks must show that not all creatures were brought forth "after their kind," as God says they were and as they certainly are now. They will never do that.

While there is a matter of 800,000,000 years difference in the claims of the experts, no one need to get uneasy for fear the friends of the Bible will be fighting science. So long as nine-tenths of the vast periods they claim, are in dispute, some of us will continue to put quotation marks around the "science" that seeks to replace revelation with opinions.

THE ARGUMENT FROM UNBORN LIFE

The author regrets that he cannot here contribute something to the exposure of the colossal hoax called "The Recapitulation Theory," but this book is written for young as well as old and though propagandists have not spared to stab the trusting faith of childhood, the arguments from unborn life must wait for another book or reach you in the books published by others.

Thirty-Three

The author does not know an eminent evolution-ist who believes there is a personal devil. If you are in doubt, surely you know that every devilish newspaper, magazine or novel that panders to sin and profits from smut, could take the devil's place in the picture.

COMPROMISES

There are as many shades and blends of evolution as there are evoluters who wish to be ORIGINAL. It naturally follows that a "science" that takes any hat for a home, will flirt with religion, and some are so impressed with the word "science" that they would

Thirty-Four

have the religion of Christ tag around after it. Evolution has a creed that its shamed devotees try to hide with borrowed morals. SELFISHNESS WINS. GRATIFY EVERY APPETITE. It sounds like a devil's "AMEN!" No need to argue this, **any cat fight will prove it.** Tennyson said:
 "Man trusted God was love indeed,
 And love Creation's final law;
 Tho' nature, red in tooth and claw
 With raven, shrieked against his creed."
No explanation or apology that denies the displeasure of God that "the earth is filled with violence," (Gen. 6:13) can serve to cloak dripping jaws with the gentleness of Christ. **Life has gone wrong; not evolved.** If you can make some nice adjustment between my devil and your God that lifts your soul, be sure **"flaming youth" will not.** Too many boys that are told their ancestry is 99 per cent brute **are making a 50 per cent average.**

This logic will give loose rein to youth for a little plunge, but its only answer to the prayer of age and frailty is: DIE AND GET OUT OF THE WAY.

If evolution has brought us through a million ages of swamp and jungle by **saving the best killers** and has given us a sense of guilt and the certainty of death and the yawning eternity, that the brutes never had, what can it offer to quiet our dread and satisfy our longing?

Do you think evolution HAS ONE LAW FOR THE TIGER AND ANOTHER FOR YOU?

When the shadows deepen, evolution has nothing for YOU but DEATH.

Cool your fever with that handful of ice.

If you think evolution was God's method, it heard no prayer and showed no mercy. When it is done with you and your little play spell is ended, will you grope in the gloom for eternal life utterly foreign to the system? How can a man who thinks he thinks hang his temporary life on a brute succession drawn

Thirty-Five

out for a half billion years and then suppose that *some shadow of himself will ride forth from his dead body on a dying gasp, to see without eyes, hear without ears and think without a brain?*

In 20 seconds—eternal life!

I do not object to any evolutionist going to heaven if evolution will leave him a heaven to go to and give him anything to go there with. If you deny the miracle of creation, what can evolution do with a corpse?

Eternal farewells, falling tears, fading flowers, silence, night!

I know there are some who believe it pleased God to breed selfishness and brutishness into man for hundreds of millions of years and then offer him heaven if he can get it out some way. Others presume that God made man by adding a part of himself to an ape's body, but what a mess they get themselves into! An ape madonna! Since the Bible says Adam was "the son of God," this is, well—you name it. It presumes that evolution has been working some 6,000 years to improve a "son of God" made "in his image." If this supposed BLEND fell, which part of the partnership takes blame?

I have no quarrel with real or hope-so science when it knows its place. God gave man a commission to "subdue" the earth and I rejoice that science can harness the untamed forces, but it must not censor revelation nor impose its hobbles on God. A science that claims to have evolved from lizards and lemurs ought to be more modest.

I want a religion older than I am, a God that neither man nor archangel can make his plans or do his thinking for him. The prophets cried, "Thus saith Jehovah"; Jesus said, "I spake not from myself"; of the Holy Spirit he said, "He shall not speak from himself." Who are these men so eager to amend the "faith once for all delivered," with a man-made message from a brain that they admit is only seven evolutionary epochs ahead of a carp?

Thirty-Six

A PARTING SHOT

Is it the truth or a lie that evolution without the trimmings that have been added to cover up its shame is really this:

TAKE WHAT YOU WANT, WHEN YOU WANT IT, ANYWHERE YOU FIND IT, ANY WAY YOU CAN GET IT?

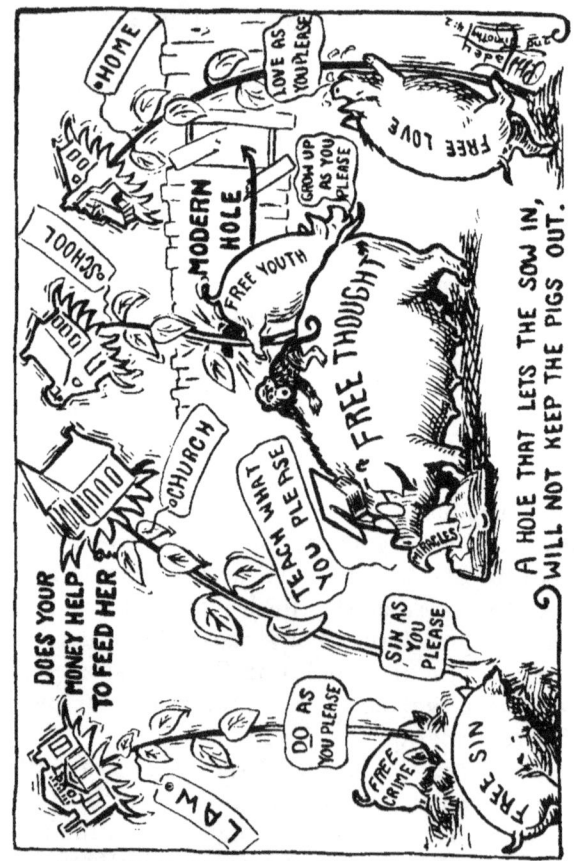

THIS IS BOTH HISTORY AND PROPHECY

"Freedom of thought" is just a pretty phrase to cover up free PROPAGANDA. Any freedom that flouts God will incubate FREE REIN and FREE TREASON. The cartoon shows the old sow that was let in to root up the "superstition" in civilization and the pigs that have followed. If you cannot see the truth of this cartoon from reading the Bible, you ought to be able to interpret the front page of your newspaper.

Arguments Against

Arguments Against

THE TOADSTOOL AMONG THE TOMBS
Copyright 1925 by B. H. Shadduck

Two

BETTER READ THIS FIRST

Some cartoons in this book, taken by themselves, might leave the impression that the author is making light of schools and scholarship. I would not willingly give offense to any school that knows its limitations or any scholarship that is reverent and humble when it approaches God.

Moses took off his shoes before the burning bush.

Uzzah died for treating the ark of God like a piece of freight.

Aaron's sons were smitten with fire because they took liberties with God.

Even the devils believe and tremble.

There are quite too many with a scholarship "gone to their head" who arrogate to themselves the right to revise the morals of the Bible, correct the prophets and keep God up-to-date and in style.

The smaller one can make his god,
THE BIGGER HE WILL SEEM BY COMPARISON.

To strip God of miracle working power, makes the stripper's deeds greater by contrast.

I do not accuse anyone of being the antichrist, but I do say that self sufficient scholarship is furnishing the precedent he will need. (2 Thes. 2:4.) **As the authority of God is weakened, human prowess will be exalted.**

In this book I am trying to show with what FLIPPANT SELF CONFIDENCE a callow student who would not know his ABCs if someone had not told him, will appoint himself judge, jury, attorney, witness and high sheriff to try appeals from the Court of God and pass upon the constitutionality of his Word. And then he modestly thanks himself for saving God's reputation.

Stimulated and sustained by a pot of coffee, he is able to dismantle a whole book of the Bible at one sitting. Death has been following the trail of this man like a hound on a track, since he drew his first breath, yet this puny death dodger feels so full of information that he thrusts himself into the councils of Infinity and cries, **"I must be reckoned with."**

A MUSHROOM GROWN TOPHEAVY NEAR HIS OWN GRAVE.

Man's mind is like a flower, it must be pollenized if there is to be fruit and the kind of fruit depends upon the kind of pollen. If this book seems independently original, distrust it. I do not know 20c worth of anything that God has overlooked. Many people who admire **butterflies**, do not realize that they are **caterpillars on dress parade.** There are many evolutionists of pleasing personality but this book is not a discussion of the butterfly side of evolution. I do not need to defame evolutionists. They do it themselves. Any man who confesses that 50 per cent of his pedigree is below the level of snakes, ought to have more sympathy than rebuke. Other books discuss the butterfly side; with kindest wishes for the brilliant individuals, bear with me while I try to show you

THE CATERPILLAR SIDE OF THE DOCTRINE.

History repeats itself. Whether God writes in his Book or on the pages of history or on the plaster of palace wall, the message is always the same. When a nation gets top heavy with conceit and puts its veto on God, he makes more homes for the bats.

Four

WHERE TWO ETERNITIES MEET

Once upon a time there was a toadstool lived among the tombs.

Even the soil through which it pushed its head was black with death—the death of other plants.

It was TOPHEAVY. It bulked large in the place where toadstools will have brains, **when evolution gets to it**. It tried to adjust all the rest of the world to its own plans and specifications, even as other toadstools do, that have brains.

It was different from toadstools that HAD BEEN.

IT WAS NEW.

If I do not impress you with the importance of NEWNESS in toadstools and others, you will miss the main idea. Other toadstools had been new, but this was new JUST THEN.

It was newer than the stars or the great California trees that began life before Jesus walked the earth in the days of his flesh. It was newer than the green moss that somehow managed to live on the gray slabs that marked the passing of great ambitions, hungers and thirsts. If it could have read on the grave stones the stories of life-fire that left only ashes and reaching hands filled with dust, it might have sensed its own passing, but it was fully occupied with its newness. Toadstools do not get old till the day after they are not. **This toadstool outranked Moses and Isaiah in the matter of newness and many "modern" people believe it MADE FEWER MISTAKES.** It is characteristic of youth to feel sorry for the ignorance of the past. I have known a father to say to his 16 year old son, "Son, you know more now than your father. You know more now than you ever will know again. I know this because at your age I was in the same fix." I am hoping the "modernists" do not enact a law to compel parents to go to school and keep up with the children. **It will discourage the children.**

Five

There are some who really believe God has waited untold centuries for a new newness to rescue him from the haze and fog that ancient people have wrapped about him.

Then why not this toadstool that *had never made a mistake?*

Some people will say this is foolishness because it took brains to hinder God from saying just what he wanted to say and revealing just what he intended to reveal. Because old brains have wrapped God in such a smother of superstition, it will take new brains to relieve him from embarrassment and *correct the mistakes of his Moses.*

Not new toadstools, but new brains that sweat out NEW THOUGHTS for the NEW DAY, must give God such a good reputation that *he can "go" in cultured society.*

But brains and toadstools *have much in common.*

MOSTLY WATER.

The provoking thing about it is, *the water in both cases is* OLD WATER that has been used for thousands of years. All that is material in a brain that is not in a toadstool could be held in a spoon, *if the wind were not blowing,* and know no more than the toadstool. The potency of brain-stuff must be nine-tenths in the water that has worn out many bodies. This would not overwork the water, for its atoms can push out the end of a steam boiler at times.

I do not mean to mock at brain.

As a central station for the marvelous telephone system of the body, it is indispensable and it serves beast about as well as man. When brain undertakes to do for man what it cannot do for beast, it is like a locomotive—valuable only while it stays on the rails and obeys the engineer. When it sets itself up as a rival of God and a pilot to the far reaches of eternity, it becomes a liability rather than an asset. When brain makes a religion for itself, it makes a fool of itself.

Arguments Against

One lone man, all by himself, half way between nurse and undertaker, presumes to run the Bible through his private mill. The porous plasters are too much porous and too much plaster. Such a man always has more to say about the fallibility of the Bible than the fallibility of himself.

Seven

GAMBLING WIH ETERNITY

A brain that will risk an eternity on its opinions, OUGHT TO BE DEPENDABLE. A brain that will gamble with other people's eternity by acting as a guide, OUGHT TO FUNCTION PERFECTLY. A brain that will take a book that purports to be the Word of God; a book that has tamed savage nations, comforted the sick and lighted the valley of the shadow of death for thousands of years; and advertises its mistakes (?), OUGHT TO BE INFALLIBLE.

But it is the most blundering thing on earth.

It is not so sure as an adding machine. A colony of ants, without schools, courts or prisons, is better governed than Chicago, because they do not have so much brain to go wrong. America with the personal liberty of ants, would collapse in anarchy, because you can never know what appalling folly a human brain may generate when it is unbridled.

As a matter of fact, the brain is least trustworthy of any organ in the body. Fever, alcohol, cocaine, morphine, hypnotism, anger and even so innocent a state as sleep, will put the mind in a condition bordering on insanity or imbecility. Then there are jazz music, flattery, fear and sex appeal that play strange pranks with minds that otherwise might not be considered feeble. It would take a page in a dictionary to define all the changing moods and whims of the brain.

There are some of us left who believe that sin in the past and the present has so sadly warped the thinking machine of man, that IT NEEDS GOD TO BE NORMAL.

God does not have brains.

That is probably why he does not make mistakes.

The word "brains" is not in the Bible. The Book does infer that man has brains, for it recognizes that there is *some source of human foolishness.* Jesus had a brain—a perfect brain—as belonging to his humiliation when he came to the

Eight

level of blood relationship with man, but *he did not rely on it.* He said, "I can of mine own self do nothing; as I hear, I judge." (John 5:30.) "Whatsoever I speak therefore, as the Father saith unto me, so I speak." (John 12:50.)

I do not object to the process that casts the mind of the pupil in the mold of the school and sends it forth like a graphophone record. That seems inevitable. John the Baptist came from the Wilderness Theological Seminary and was little more than "A VOICE." More than most men admit, we are like parrots—our wisdom is second hand. The point I would emphasize is that the prophet of God must speak for God, and somewhere back of the message there must be the Word of God.

There is very little original thought today and this is well, for human thought ferments and men get drunk on it—at times. The prophets of God were the ECHO-MEN of God. Knowledge that begins with God and is relayed from man to man is scriptural. (2 Tim. 2:2.) If any man presumes to invent a message, "Let him be accursed." (Gal. 1:8,12.)

GOD'S TESTIMONY

God has ever shown a kind of contempt for mere brain-wisdom. When man has gone his limit—self guided—he has only reached God's classification of "fool." "For the wisdom of this world is foolishness with God."

When they asked Jesus about greatness in the kingdom, he set a little child in their midst, though there were brains enough in that crowd to fill a garbage can.

Facing such facts as these, one would think that if a man had a barrel of brains pickled by the most recent university process, he would be very humble and apologetic in imposing his own limitations on the Eternal God, but instead of meekness, these revelation inspectors and adjusters, fix up an alibi for God and pronounce spurious or outworn, those parts of the Holy Scriptures that they think will injure God's reputation with the fast traveling younger set. They don't want God to be left behind in their parade, and if the restraint-hating NEW people will not adjust themselves to the old time revelation of God, why, in that case, they will adjust revelation to *"The revolt of youth."*

If God educated his angels in some EGOLOGICAL SEMINARIES, they might so modernize heaven that some of our Brainitarians would be willing to go there.

Is it not true that 9999 out of every 10,000 who profess evolvo-ism repeat the say-so of someone else? It takes four kinds of 'ology to furnish theories for evolutionists. If some quick thinker insists that we accept the say-so of the Bible, we answer that the prophecies of the Bible COME TRUE and evolution cannot grow one feather on a frog. Is there a prophet of God in the picture?

Ten

THE DONATION PARTY (Ex. 32:3)

"Modernism" is a kind of donation party on much the same plan and for much the same purpose as the collection that Aaron gathered to make a substitute for the "mistakes of Moses." If you do not know the sources of this modern anti-Moses movement, *at least you can see the "NEW" calf.* In Aaron's case even as today, there was an anti-Moses movement and God seemed to be losing out with the "thinkers", until an "adjustment" was made. Now we have a newer NEWNESS that is calculated to relieve God from embarrassment in the presence of great learning and excuse him from responsiblitiy for the mistakes of Moses. It would seem that God has been so busy correcting the mistakes of others for thousands of years that his Book must needs wait for fresh new brains that are the very latest caper of evolution, to tell the befogged world that God DID NOT DO what they think he COULD NOT and WOULD NOT DO what they think he OUGHT NOT.

Reader: If you are tempted, as I have been, to use caustic language to denounce such doings, remember that steam that escapes through the safety valve would do better pushing a piston. Better invest a dollar in literature that will save your neighbor. Still, one wonders what Jesus and John the Baptist would say in these days.

Not content with fixing up God's reputation for him so that he need not be ashamed among people of profound scholarship, they have fixed up something like an ape mammy to be a proxy for God until the first man was old enough to be weaned. As one might expect, they insist that this cub or whelp or litter of a brute dam was such a low down mongrel that his race had to be filtered through 500,000 years (more or less) of selfish struggle and combat to elevate man to the level of an educated ex-cannibal or (if you like it better) to where he would spit in the face of Christ and mock him while he died. If evolutionists prefer a later period when women and children were killed with poison gas, they are welcome.

Now that we have a thousand drugs to stimulate and stupefy and regulate and rectify us in our superiority, THE

Eleven

MONKEYS ARE TO GIVE US ANOTHER LIFT. Science can now graft portions of monkey into man. If this does not help, it will at least insure a return ticket to apedom. Why not graft highly evolved human brain into gorillas and see if our cultivated "NEW" tops that yield such NEW TOUGHTS, will not do even better on a more vigorous stump? In that much acclaimed book entitled, "The Earth Speaks to Bryan by Henry Fairfield Osborn," that eminent evolutionist says on page 70, *"As a race we are rapidly dying out."* (Underscore it with red ink.)

Good for one trip
MONKEY TO MAN and Return

The earth ought to know; it has seen other races evolvofinished. Is our coming extinction the work of evolution? Can a race that destroys itself be trusted to make over the Bible to fit its own wisdom? Why not delay our extinction and speed up our successors by taking evolution out of the schools and concentrating it in the monkey house?

Reader: I am well aware that some agents of this shifting "science" are now saying that man did not descend from any present-day ape. Well, what difference does it make whether we are ape-orphaned or not? If we must go back 2,000,000 years to find a basis for a family reunion at the zoo, then it means we have descended from something 2,000,000 years lower down than an up-to-date monkey. Why should we be snobbish about modern apes, seeing evolution has worked as long with them as with us and they are also sons and daughters of the (r)evolution?

In denying creation and miracles, "modernists" relieve their God from overwork. Some of them very consistently excuse him from any supernatural efforts on their behalf after death, while others hope he will take whatever gets away from the undertaker and make a glorified saint of it *in a minute, without help from the brutes.* They expect to be evolved from a corpse to angel level in a minute and stay for eternity. It does not occur to them that this is too much speed for a system that takes millions of years **to make a**

Twelve

man that can hold the job only 70 years.

It is still worse logic to presume that a God-driven evolution would work for geological ages to make a brute that cannot sin, into a man who brings on himself the "fierceness and wrath of Almighty God" because he has some brute left in him. It is a crime against common sense to teach that it pleased God to put a premium on selfishness and give a bonus of mates and progeny to the best killers and then damn his man for acting like his God-rewarded ancestors.

Reader: You can perhaps understand why certain church papers that call evolution "God's method," refuse to advertise these books.

Do not expect Christian evolutionists to be consistent; it can't be done.

THE TWO IDEAS ARE MUTUALLY EXCLUSIVE.

There are some who try to be consistent by discredititng anything disagreeable in the Bible and recasting their faith to fit their fad. If miracles are allowed, God might really make a man as like or unlike other creatures as he pleased. If the fall of man is acknowledged, then man was better when God made him than he is now and that would be evolvo-heresy. If they admit that God manifests "fierce anger" towards the results of a process he has personally directed, *it would be a confession that he is less pleased with evolution than they are.* So they have given their Bible "treatment" to make it more flexible.

This is all very satisfying to the obliging mind that can see evolution (where it is not) in a rosebud, a cradle or a Sunday School but cannot see the "dirty work" in swamp and jungle. *Evolutionists need a brutal selfishness in their* PROCESS, *that they disown in their* RELIGION. They insist on an ancestry with 4 kinds of tails but it grieves them to see 4 tails in a picture of their theory.

EVOLUTION NEEDS A DEVIL

If, for the sake of discussion, we admit that evolution is a fact, its one great commandment is, DIE AND MAKE A

Does any bright school boy believe it is good evolution for a tom cat to hate his enemies, but a boy must love his? Evolutionists defend a selfish brutal struggle in their SYSTEM that they rebuke in their SUNDAY SCHOOL. How can a good doctor be a good evolutionist when he helps the unfit to survive?

Fourteen

DINNER FOR OTHERS. If it prolongs life, it is for the same reason that a farmer saves a brood sow from the knife. If one little baby toad comes to maturity from the thousand eggs the mother left in the pool, it is only that another crop may be ready for the slaughter next year. I can understand why the men who framed the theory of evolution, left out the idea of a personal God, but I cannot understand how anyone can explain deviltry without a devil.

Old fashioned faith sees in the pitiless reign of tooth and claw, a proof that life has gone wrong and death is the doing of the devil "that hath the power of death." (Heb. 2:14.) If evolutionists did recognize "the prince of this world" as a factor in the world's trouble, they would be forced to *rate him as a good devil,* because torture is presumed to bring about the survival of the fittest; else why do we suffer from fleas, mosquitoes and other angels of evolution?

THE BEAR STORY (II. Kings 2:24)

The "modernist" excuses the horrors of brute struggle as justified, if they help evolution, and then with amazing inconsistency, his sensitive soul is shamed and shocked with Bible stories that indicate God determined *some* survivals. Just now, they are much displeased (as Ingersoll was) with the Bible story of two bears that very effectively scratched a gang of young hoodlums for mocking a prophet of God. Hidden away under their apparent compassion for the hoodlums, there is an eagerness to find a weak spot in the Bible.

If these bears were only EVOLUTIONARY BEARS giving an EVOLUTIONARY TREATMENT to hoodlums that were not strictly Class A, to bring about the SURVIVAL of the fittest, *their behavior would be only rude helpfulness.* Rather odd, isn't it, that *this* bear performance could not possibly be justified, but all the bear and wolf and snake killings for unnumbered centuries of supposed evolution are sacred *if they fit into a theory that discredits the Bible?*

Jesus said something about "blind guides that could not tolerate gnats but could swallow camels.

Fifteen

All the pillage and plunder of the innocent that the Bible blames on the devil, these chief guides would put under the benediction of God, with their favorite phrase, "IT IS GOD'S METHOD," and the little echo-guides repeat, "God's method." I have heard it so often that when an adjuster strikes a pose of pity for the ignorant, I know what is coming.

Perhaps you wonder how men who make their living by thinking for other people, can juggle with common sense this way, but what else can they do? There is a pleasing figure in Isaiah of a bed that humped a man to get into it and a cover that pulled loose one place when it was tucked in at another. Long ago, FREEthinkers rejected miracles in order to have a brain-size god that would do things according to their program. Their creed was so limited that when they rested on it, their ETERNITY HAD TO STICK OVER. Evolution was seized upon to cover the beginning of life; they left the other end to the undertaker. They never pretended that evolution had anything to offer old age but DEATH. The great agnostic inventors of evolution who predicted that their theories would destroy Christianity, never dreamed that their philosophy would become a pillar in the temple of an IMPROVED (?) "christianity." They never guessed that they would some day be reckoned the forerunners of an ADJUSTED gospel.

LAW AND LIBERTY

Law without liberty is bondage.

Liberty without law is anarchy.

If this is not clear, you had better skip this paragraph.

The law that science talks about is God's HABIT of doing things. A miracle is God's exercise of FREEDOM FROM BONDAGE to habit. SCIENCE is man's discovery of some of these habits and REVELATION is God's testimony of his freedom. *When there can be no variaiton from habit, there can be* NO CHOICE. (Is that clear?) If there is no possible choice there can be no FREE WILL. To be

Sixteen

all habit and no free will, means a machine, an idiot or a slave. Now one way of denying the existence of a God is to assume that he may have started what he cannot stop. He can have no freedom if his will that flowed when the worlds were made, *has frozen up for eternity.* If there can be no miracle, then law is superior to God, and if he made laws that are his masters, he is not RULER, but RULED. Only by playing fast and loose with logic can one presume a personal God has made a code of blind, merciless, tireless, inevitable laws that man can harness and make work, but God cannot command them, "Peace, be still!"

Now a keen school boy can see that it does not help matters to presume that God can do a little miracle, but he cannot do a great one. It is trying to crawl out through a small hole to ASSUME a knowledge that God WOULD NOT work a miracle, for that assumes you know about as well how to manage a world as he does.

Do not be deceived by the fog and smoke and smother of words; *back of* all the bluff and bluster and stampeding of the new religion that skulks behind evolution is just one real question, COULD GOD MAKE MAN WITHOUT BIRTH? *It is wholly a question of miracle.*

JUST SUPPOSE

Suppose that we accept at face value all the claims and guesses and comparisons and suppositions that evolutionists offer as evidence of brute ancestry, *such testimony could only create a presumption, unless you deny that God could create directly from the dust.* If they find a dozen "missing links," no one could possibly KNOW that any one of them hooked onto Adam. If they could prove that in the past there lived the Neanderthaler, the Heidelberger, the Eonthropus, Pithecanthropus and Humbug-us, WHAT OF IT? *Could not God make another one as like and as different as he pleased?* Suppose God looked the world over today and decided that our race would die (as evolutionists say these races did), WOULD THERE BE ANYTHING TO HINDER GOD USING THE SAME GENERAL PATTERN TO MAKE

Seventeen

SOMETHING BETTER FROM UNTAINTED MATERIAL? On the other hand it is *unreasonable* to suppose that God would *use the material of a dying race to build a race that would live,* EITHER THEN OR NOW? Can a God big enough to run a universe, make a man out of stone as Matt. 3:9 says he can? If he did, would any BLOOD TEST or COMPARATIVE ANATOMY or OLD BONES prove that he did not? (I wish I could get an answer to this.)

WAS MAN THE FATHER OF HIS "ANCESTORS"?

At the time this is written (1925) the most recent discovery that upsets the schedule of evolutionists, is the pictograph of a dinosaur in the Hava Supai canyon in Arizona, not many miles from petrified footprints of these animals. The significance claimed for this find is that it proves man lived long before the anthropoid "ancestors" that "science" has donated to him and long before the "missing links" were missed. Several eminent "ancestor" and "link" makers have explained this find by saying what is enclosed in these brackets (   ). They find it convenient to ignore evidence that they cannot use.

I am asked if this will not also discredit the Bible claim that man has lived only since Adam. I have repeatedly called attention to the fact that there is nothing in the Bible to deny that creatures may have lived in the far past that used tools ,fire and language. The point I emphasize is that THEY WERE NOT MEN—certainly not God's image-men. The Bible does mention the Nachash and Nephilim and their behavior indicates that they were MAN-LIKE. I do not concede that there were prehistoric races; I only emphasize the fact that, if there were, they do not disprove the creation of Adam. Gen. 2:20 might mean that while a mate for Adam was possible, yet there was none "meet" (suitable) in the mind of God.

If God can work a miracle, he can make another man so like me that my dog will follow him off, yet there be no kinship. There can never be evidence, in the absence of witnesses, that God *did not do* what he *could have done.*

Of course there may be such an array of OPINIONS that God is out-voted, but little drops of opinion do not make an ocean of fact. The consistent evolutionist must deny miracles or admit that he MAY BE mistaken. As a body, evolutionists are slipping as fast as the skids will let them slide to an anti-miracle religion, and an anti-Bible god. *If you do not accept this as history, take it as prophecy.*

Here is a question for debate.

Resolved: That a miracle working God could have directly created man as like unto and as different from other creatures as the assured facts of science demand. Will any

Eighteen

sensible man take the negative?

It is not even clever dodging to say as some do, **"He could do it, but he did not."** Once it is admitted that God could have done it, it becomes a question of PROBABILITY rather than science, and ought not to be decided by votes. God has been willing for thousands of years to have his people believe in creation and miracles and it is rather late in the world's history to tell God we are a self appointed jury with a verdict to guide him in making a man some thousands of years ago. Even if God were bound to respect the wishes of the majority and be governed by our INITIATIVE AND REFERENDUM, yet it would be the quintessence of folly to vote on a program of what has already happened. No doubt that some African tribes would vote that water could not turn solid, but that would not keep water from freezing at the North Pole BEFORE THEY VOTED. Really it is safest not to hand God his resignation dated 6000 years ago, nor tell him how he had to do a thing after he has done it.

Infidels have known for a century what some Christians ignore, that evolution has no place for a miracle working, personal God.

Let me say to young Christians that a God who is reduced to skull-size, is quite too feeble to get you past the undertaker.

In the face of the fact that science can never know that God did not make ONE MAN AND ONE WOMAN, some pious souls who are overawed by anything that parades as science, say to me, "How will your teachings look a hundred years from now when evolution is as certainly established as the law of gravitation, and how will you answer to God for the youth you have misled?"

Well, if they dig up Adam's autobiography after I am gone and he says he well remembers his dam was something like an ape and his mother-in-law was some sort of gorilla; if they find the personal diary of Moses and he says that God framed the "rib story" to keep his people more ignorant than their heathen neighbors WHO DID ACCEPT ANI-

Nineteen

MAL KINSHIP, then let someone who loves me go out to the monkey house and apologize for my snobbery.

If the time comes that evolution vindicates itself by restoring the 4 tails they say our ancestors lost and the birth-control advocates order their families from a monkey cata-log, then let someone write on my tombstone, "He believed the Bible too much." I cannot fear to meet Jesus believing as he did. He never warned us against believing the Holy Scriptures, but he did warn repeatedly against false prophets who would RISE and SEDUCE. *That means something new, does it not?* He warned against false Christs. *A false Christ must be a NEW Christ.* In the face of such warnings, is it safer to believe the prophets or the fellows who would put them in eclipse?

Let us reverse the question. If it turns out that man came fresh from the hand of God and you have pleaded* for an ancestry that goes back to reptiles and beyond and you have insisted that while under a mother's heart, before you were born, you again passed through the FORM of a reptile; what will you say to an insulted God when "he treadeth the winepress of the fierceness and wrath of Almighty God"?

Let hesitating youth be well advised that present styles in "scientific" ancestry do not stop with putting reptiles in your pedigree millions of years ago, but they insist that before you were born, you passed through REPTILE form in your development. This is a part of the abominable "recapitulation" theory that ought to shame a devil. Men have been shot for insults that were polite in comparison. There is a book bearing the imprint of a great university that shows a picture indicating that we have descended from some ancient dam that was equipped to nurse a litter of SEVENTEEN.

Would it be humanly possible for me to say meaner things about evolutionists than they say about themselves? Would it? And to think they teach that the Son of God on his human side was descended from a crawling reptile and

  The author has known a speaker to plead for the acceptance of evolution, WITH TEARS.

Twenty

that the angels heralded the coming of a babe that was but a few months removed from gill slits.

Again and again the weak brethren among evolutionists who feel they need some faith to go with their doubts, tell us they believe the Bible but interpret it differently. They argue that the Bible statements of the shape of the earth were figures of speech and that the story of creation is also figurative language. This reasoning is so shallow that we think a bright school boy can see through it.

1st. No reinterpretation can be honest that makes a figure of speech teach the **opposite** of the literal statement.

2nd. There are statements in the Bible that make a 4 cornered flat world literally impossible. See Job 26:7, Prov. 8:27, Isa. 40:22, and the prophecy of Jesus that when he comes it will be day in one place, night in another. (A fair inference from Luke 17:34-36.)

3rd. The circle of the earth was settled by going around it both ways, but evolutionists can neither make reptiles into birds nor birds into reptiles.

4th. The questions of sin, repentance, forgiveness, atonement, judgment, heaven and hell, do not depend on the shape of the earth. They do depend upon whether man climbed from a brute ancestry UP or fell from a God ancestry DOWN. (See Luke 3:38.) There needs to be no bloody cross to save a man from GETTING BETTER.

5th. The Bible is the ONLY ancient book that did tell the literal truth about the world; on the other hand, the Bible would be 5,000 years behind the ancient heathen, if evolution is a fact, because PAGANISM ACCEPTED ANIMAL KINSHIP LONG, LONG AGO.

Let us freely admit that there is poetry and figure of speech in the Bible, but parables are meant to be PARALLELS not **barriers of** truth. A literal black vulture cannot be reinterpreted to mean the song of a white humming bird. It takes more than a metaphorical twist to make the story of creation mean evolution; it **requires contradiction.**

Can the story of man's fall be made to mean that he went up?

Can literal disobedience mean figurative loyalty?

Is the Garden of Eden a poetical name for a dirty cave, littered with bones?

Twenty-One

Can the story of Eve mean she was not made from a rib but was a freak yearling of anthropoid apes, who was too "smart" to associate with her mammy?

Is the story of God's grief when the world went corrupt, a parable meaning he was overjoyed that it turned out better than he expected?

Is the story of the curse that followed sin, only a loving hoax to satisfy ignorant people until they could understand it by the name "evolution"?

Is the devil only a sacred myth to explain "deviltry" until man could understand it is only the reptile "hang-over" that remains in us?

If you can interpret Genesis as a kind of PUNCH AND JUDY show to please childish people, why not interpret hell as the front entrance to heaven?

If evolution is God's method, why not presume it will continue to be, and heaven will be an eternal torture of the weak by the strong?

EVOLUTIONARY HEAVEN AND HELL

"Heaven on earth" may well be described as the state of man when God's perfect will is done in him. The heaven of God must be that same condition made to fit eternity and infinity. "Hell on earth" is that state of man when God is most defied and ignored. Hell to come must be the full harvest of such sowing. *Now what kind of heaven and hell would fit evolution?* If evolution has a heaven, it ought to be *an eternal and infinite multiplication of the process when tooth and claw and horn and famine and pestilence were doing their best* (or worst). Its streets might well be paved with skulls, its rivers red, its music the hiss and howl and scream of the jungle.

If evolution has a hell, it must be *a continuation of the life of its backsliders intensified.* Has some life defied evolution? All parasites, as lice, ticks, fleas, scale and even such creatures as whales, are *listed by evolutionists as degenerates* that have left a higher level for an easier life. THE ONES THAT DID NOT BACKSLIDE HAVE TO BE TORTURED BY THE ONES THAT DID.

Twenty-Two

After thinking it over, I believe I would rather go to evolution's hell *where the system is a failure,* than to its heaven where its horrors are magnified by infinity and eternity.

Do not be deceived by modern efforts to put a goody-goody mantle on evolution; it is no more Christian now than when infidels accepted it as the foe of Christianity. To love enemies and return good for evil would be an apostate evolution, *utterly false to a system they say depended on the weak being crushed by the strong, in the carnival of death that helped God make a man.* If anyone wishes to deny this, let him first explain how evolution could accomplish the survival of the fittest if it showed mercy to the unfit. *(As a matter of fact, the ones most evolved (?) are the ones nearest extinction.)*

Let us face the brutal facts. Any bright farmer's boy who has seen horses tortured by flies will be slow to accept the teacher's decree that it is God's method of making a man. If this is his plan, then why do we pray, "Thy will be done in earth as it is in heaven"? *Is it done this way in heaven, only more so?* We live in a world of cruelty. Something has gone wrong with God's creation. (See Gen. 6:11.) If "modernists" wish to abolish the devil and put the responsibility on evolution, why do they try to disinfect their barnyard creed with borrowed piety?

Whether you call it the work of the devil or evolution, God was utterly disgusted with "all flesh" in Noah's time and if you think Jesus was any better satisfied with the "progress" of man, read his words pregnant with doom. "Ye are the sons of them which killed the prophets. Fill ye up the measure of your fathers. Ye serpents, ye generation of vipers, how can ye escape the damnation of hell?"

If any man, who admits he is more intelligent than believers in the direct creation of man, insists on reptile ancestry, HE OUGHT TO BE ACCOMMODATED. Ever since Adam and Eve sought an excuse for sin, man has been prone

Twenty-Three

to welcome any theory *that he is doing as good as could be expected.*

WHAT SHALL BE FINAL AUTHORITY?

If you make *science your **supreme court**,* be assured that *it will decide all miracles are* UNCONSTITUTIONAL. When this is written, men are making much sport of the sun and moon standing still for Joshua. One writer who is advertised *daily* as "The highest paid editorial writer in the world," has taken 3 or 4 minutes to demolish that story. He wisely informs us that if the earth had stopped (making the sun seem to stop), the water and atmosphere would keep going and wreck the earth's surface. It seems not to have occurred to him that a God who could stop the earth *might have presence of mind enough to stop* ALL OF IT. In the past, men have taken a lifetime to discredit the Bible, but now we have men who can fill a pipe and empty a Bible story *between puffs.* The story of Joshua and the sun has been denied and defended a thousand times yet some who revel in the denials are totally ignorant of the defense.

Every day we speak of material things as "SOLID." Science says they are made up of particles in commotion. We call them "solid" because they are *solid to our experiences.* The Bible was written in man's language so man could understand it, and states its facts in terms of man's experience, just as we do every day. I do not know how that day was lengthened and I do not need to know; all that would be necessary would be for God to curve the rays of light coming from the sun or slow them up to snail's pace.

Some well meaning people fear that some mistakes may have gotten into the Bible. I have no occasion to defend translations, but I insist that God is bound to make good every promise, prophecy and warning in the original writings he has stood sponsor for through the centuries. If a rich man employs a secretary to write his checks and the secretary overwrites the amounts, that rich man must protest the

---

*We use the word science as it is commonly understood.

Twenty-Four

mistakes or pay the checks. For hundreds of years, the critics have been advising God of the mistakes (?) and he seems satisfied to let them continue. IF THERE ARE MISTAKES, THEY ARE ALL IN MY FAVOR and God must make good.

I will not make a fetish of science—either real or guess-so.

I hope I am not unmindful of its power to bless; even as I am not blind to its power to curse the race. I would not care to take the affirmative in a debate on this question, *"Resolved: That modern science has blessed more than it has cursed and saved more life than it has destroyed or prevented."* Great statesmen and evolutionists are saying, *"The next world war will destroy civilization."* As for me, I rely more upon the prophecies of Jesus than on the predictions and diplomacy of statesmen, but this is a good place to ask, IF SCIENCE HAS BECOME A MENACE TO CIVILIZATION, IS IT A SAFE GUIDE IN RELIGION? Science is as ready to sell itself to war lords to destroy the living and to selfish couples to prevent others being born as it is to prolong the life of a dangerous criminal. The crooked lawyer invokes the testimony of science on behalf of his murdering client and the shameless libertine, steeped in vice, calls on science to make debauchery safe.

Of course, there is a blessed side to science, but it is utterly helpless when the little candle flame that men call *life,* flickers in the night wind that makes for the timeless sea, *and goes out.* Some day science at its best will stand by your bed and finger your pulse and whisper to the watchers, "I can do no more." In that hour it will be well to know a God beside whom science is a puny putterer. It will be a poor time to try to see God through the holes men have made in his Book. If I am conscious in that hour, I want to say to my soul, *"Science was not your god in life; you need not obey it now and* STAY DEAD." I want to say to the tired body, "Sleep here with science till the shout of Jesus and the trump of God shall recreate his image-man from the insensate dust and loose him from its limitations forever."

FROM LEFT TO RIGHT THE BED-FELLOWS ARE:— "CHRISTIAN" LEADER (SO CALLED), UNITARIAN, AGNOSTIC, ANARCHIST

When the author was a boy, infidels welcomed evolution as a foe to Christianity and an assurance that they had nothing to fear from a personal God, but only anarchists believed that survival by brute force was good for society. Now I have lived to see clergymen help Darrow discredit the Bible.

THE HEAVEN SIGN ON THE HELL ROAD. You will not see all that is in this picture at first glance. Read Matt. 7:13. Notice the portable church, the changed signs and the caste lines that classify sin. Many people feel secure if the majority is with them.

The Toadstool Among the Tombs

This picture parable well represents the plaything religion that is being offered as a substitute for the bloody cross, the broken tomb and the "day of wrath." There is nothing about it to annoy a sinner. It lacks one thing—the tree needs a lightning rod.

We had a name for the youth on the left but withheld it to avoid giving someone pain. The figure well represents the company of students, some of whom had not yet cut all their teeth, that wired Darrow their congratulations that he was fighting the big "boob" (Bryan).

We have a number of names for this cartoon. Why not call it "THE APE THAT PITCHED HIS TENT TOWARD SODOM"? They have unvelled the image of an ape in a New York church (see Jocko-Homo) and we here picture one in the shadow of the same kind of church. If the ape understands graft, "political pressure", and exploiting of sex, he will not care to evolve.

Arguments Against

HISTORY and PROPHECY

Human passions are restrained by civil law which is always based on man's notion of divine law. When the authority of the Bible is destroyed, the destroyers will be the first ones overwhelmed by the flood. No mere umbrella of optimism will stay the deluge.

Bible believers have dared and double dared evolutionists to answer the things we do say. The author has offered to meet any acknowledged leader among evolutionists, on the platform or on the printed page, but the only answer he has been able to get is A REFUSAL TO ADVERTISE THESE BOOKS. He offers to print a book and give half the pages to the first accredited leader that offers, but they would rather fight their straw man.

Arguments Against

This is a cartoon that was crowded out of the book PUDDLE TO PARADISE. Similar cartoons in that book have not been popular with evolutionists. We do not see why they are annoyed by a picture parable that portrays the ancestry of man as they proclaim it. In this picture, we have only put together the "missing links" and the links that they haven't missed and made an ancestral chain. Somehow, they do not like it.

Reader: If you have read this book with profit, why not tell your friends about it? There are two others at the same price; they have thus far been sold without profit. By sending for them you help us to help others.

I have been most fortunate in my helpers. F.W. Alden, 602 Madison St., Waukesha, Wis., makes both cartoons and etchings. He has been patient, painstaking and quick to understand. If you need either sketches or plates made, write him. P. H. Kadey is a clever cartoonist-evangelist. His work speaks for itself. If you need an evangelist that can illustrate his preaching, write him at 819 16th St., Port Huron, Mich.

The first name selected for this book was "THE AGE OF TREASON". The artist knew nothing of this. Imagine the author's surprise when he saw "AGE OF T-REASON" in the design prepared for cover by Mr. Alden. Can you see it?

This is the new Tabernacle for the New Day. When it is occupied, it some times shelters a pot of gray matter that is reckoned to be a safer guide than the God portrayed in the Bible.

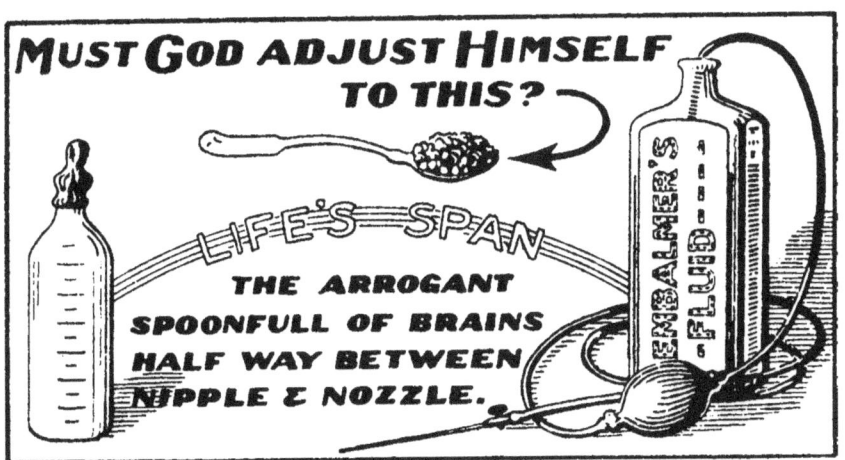

Arguments Against

FIRST EDITION 20 CENTS

THE GEE-HAW
OF THE MODERN JEHU
BY B. H. SHADDUCK
Ph. D.

Arguments Against

When we planned a picture fable to symbolize the inconsistency of men who try to drive the contradictory theories of brute cruelty for the past, and fawning mercy for the future, as the method of God, we wished to use an angel-like figure to symbolize such mercy, but, thinking it might give affront to angels if the reader misunderstood the picture, we chose the horse. We later used the first plan in the cover design and ask the reader to regard it as a representation of mercy mis-hitched. Interpret a similar figure in the book, in the same way.

Copyright 1928 by B. H. SHADDUCK

Arguments Against

A STATEMENT OF THE CASE

This is not meant to be a battle of brains.

It may be fortunate for me that it does not need to be.

Herein I call attention to the contradictions of a man of intellectual brilliance and I would not leave the impression that it is a battle of giants, unless we assume that this man is twins under one hat and is at war with himself.

Let me waive any claim to equal scholarship; IT IS YOUR BRAIN THAT I WOULD USE IN THIS DISCUSSION. Because there are some who scold at my presumption in daring to review the utterances of great men, let us concede that these men have twice as many encyclopedias and have read them three times as much.

If a great man teaches one theory on Sunday and an opposite theory on Monday, very ordinary people may contrast BOTH theories on Tuesday.

THIS IS WRITTEN ON TUESDAY; YOU CAN SEE THE INCONSISTENCY OF HUMAN GREATNESS ANY DAY.

It appears that the bigger the brain, the more places there are for cracks in it and the longer the dog, the more likely it is that one end will be coming back before the other end gets there. Really, there is no reason why common folks should be overawed by any imposing wisdom that is made out of bread and meat. Let me point out some basic facts.

WE LIVE IN A WORLD OF SLAUGHTER.

It requires no array of scholarship to decide that this is a world of KILL OR BE KILLED. We may make it stronger and say it is a world of kill AND be killed. Some man has written a book entitled, "The Lives of the Hunted," without telling his readers that everything from louse to elephant is hunted. Every leaf and blade of grass is hunting ground for killers and if one considers the uncounted millions of crawling, hopping, buzzing creatures in one stretch of meadow, two questions may arise.

How many of the babies of these creatures will live to maturity?

How many of those that are mature will live out the year?

Then if you are not too busy smelling the flowers, a third question may persist.

WHAT KIND OF GOD OR DEVIL IS DELIGHTED WITH THESE CONDITIONS OF LIFE?

Of course, I believe the sixth chapter of Genesis and if you do not, at least your common sense can decide that if this is the method that God has loved and brooded over for a billion years, then fawning mercy is not in his make-up; HE IS A GOD TO BE AFRAID OF.

If, as the Book says, God is grieved with this murderous world and if Jesus is a part of God's plan to make earth like heaven, then no flights of foggy eloquence can sanctify any alleged evolution, nor can gushing optimism make God to truckle with sin.

Because this man is just one among thousands, and *not the first one*, to insist on an animal hell for the past and presume on a public heaven for the future, I do not make it personal by announcing his name. The reader can find a man in almost every community to whom this discussion will apply.

THE GEE-HAW OF THE MODERN JEHU
BY B. H. SHADDUCK, PH. D.

Author of the Jocko-Homo series of books, "Seven Thunders of Millennial Dawn" and other papers.

I am told that an ardent evolutionist who is a leader in the "modern" religious movement, recently broadcasted the following:

"I do not believe that God will ever strike down the hand raised to him for mercy, either in this world or the next."

Dramatically stated, isn't it?

Calls to mind Uncle Tom before Simon Legree or Antonio at the mercy of Shylock. It poses the characters in such a way that *God will lose the applause of the galleries, if He denies it.* It borrows the methods of the criminal lawyer who plays upon the maudlin sympathies of a jury to make them believe the criminal is the one who is being wronged.

On the surface, it looks like a pretty compliment paid to a God who has been too modest to speak for himself, but really it amounts to an announcement of what the speaker would do if he had charge of God's mercy. It is so easy for politicians to be generous with other people's money and for obliging preachers to vote large appropriations of mercy that is not at their disposal.

Most of us are the descendants of people, who, in the degenerate past, worshipped idols of some sort and there is yet in many of us a proneness to risk our eternity on the guess-so or hope-so of some man who has been highly exalted by his fellows. I freely concede the greatness of this man's intellect, but I remind you that the bigger the belfry, the more places there are for bats. In saying this, I mean no disrespect for this or any other great man; I am thinking of that wisest of men—Solomon—who proved that he was also equipped for being about as big a fool as any. Many times in history, great wisdom and great folly have played tag under the same hat. Sometimes a bee knows the way home better than a philosopher. I concede the wide sweep of those intellects that have such an expanse that there is room enough for cat-fight-ism and dove-love-ism to amble about in the same brain and not bump into each other.

The Cradle-Throne of "New" Conceptions. Are new conceptions saving the world faster than the old? Watch and see.

The Gee-HAW of the Modern Jehu

There is nothing really new about this eagerness to quiet the fears of uneasy sinners and some who would like to take on a little more sin. It seems that Mother Eve had a visitor who convinced her that the penalty for sin was greatly overstated. The novelty of this movement to unscare sin lovers is that it comes from people who *offer us one kind of God to get us here and another kind to get us away.*

Heresy is always inconsistent, but oh what an intellectual straddle it requires to believe that *man can ride in with the apes, snap his fingers at God and ride out with the angels. One needs to be a mental acrobat to believe that God planned the survival of the fittest for the jungle and a survival of the misfits for heaven.* It is no wonder that atheists are jubilant. No wonder a bunch of college boys made a throne for a stuffed ape with Bibles, in the year of our Lord 1927.*

If you think they can explain all this, loan them the book and see.

(Reader: We have coaxed them, dared them, even tried to hire them to explain their contradictions and the only answer I can get is that *we are not scientists* and they refuse to discuss it with us.)

Well, to some of us who had only human ancestors, it looks like a hopeless contradiction, to assume that God skimmed the cream or scum of a lower order of life to make a higher order, and skimmed and skimmed and skimmed the skimmings until he had a super-ape that knew enough to tie a stone on the end of a stick and cook his neighbor before eating him; then *when His masterpiece degenerates until it is hell for the man to live with himself,* He promotes him to fellowship with the angels in thirty seconds, if he knows *how to swindle God.*

It takes an education that is beyond me to understand how the same God would make every drop of water a crystal slaughter house and every leaf an altar dedicated to death in a billion year process to push man's brain two inches farther from his "gill-slits" than is the ape's; and then jump the man who resists HIM to angel level because He cannot bear to see anyone unhappy.

You need not expect them to explain it. It is easier to assume that we are ignorant.

*See "Alibi, Lullaby, By-by."

Arguments Against

Five million centuries to lift simple plasm to the level of rats and weasels and torturing insects and man, and after all the evolution and culture and science and legislation, it is not safe for a ten-year-old girl to walk the streets of a great city alone after dark. Then, after man has hardened himself by refusing mercy and has damned himself by resisting God, to *sell him heaven for a gesture,* is a sort of mercy that utterly spoils the theory of evolution.

Evidently Jesus was not satisfied with what the supposed evolution *has done* for man or what the supposed fawning mercy *will do* for him. If there was an evolution, he ought to have known it; if there are complimentary tickets that will admit heaven-haters to heaven, he ought to have known it, yet he said, *"Ye must be born again."*

It is said that a mother oyster may produce as many as sixty million eggs in one season. By the law of averages, not one in a million can come to maturity, and those that do, soon come to grief. If we consider all the creatures, visible and invisible, that have met death in the supposed process that finally vexed the earth with a man (Gen. 6:6), then evolution has cost more lives than there are sands on the shore, drops in the sea and leaves in the forest.

And look at the mess we have!

Geological ages, to go the bloody path from amoeba to God-defying man so that all the mercy unknown to the process may be lavished on such a man *after he has lost the place to put it.*

I know the earth is "filled with violence"; God said so. Unless the statements of Gen. 6 are true and the appalling waste of life is contrary to his original plan—that is to be restored some day (Is. 11:6)—then there is nothing in the struggle of life among the brutes to suggest mercy *either here or hereafter.* Death is an enemy to be destroyed (I. Cor. 15:26). If God will let the world suffer for its corruption *now,* there is nothing in experience to argue that He will not let wilfully impenitent rebels live with themselves when His kingdom comes—a kingdom that will be as unlike the carnival of horrors that they call "evolution," as it will be unlike the hoped-for heavenly anarchy that they call "mercy."

Of course, this easy-escape doctrine will be **popular**

The Gee-HAW of the Modern Jehu

Please accept our assurances that we do not use the figures of a dachshund to suggest either the pedigree or character of our evolutionary friends. As the tail is the logical conclusion of even a long dog, we suggest to those who deny the embryonic heaven in the front end of the Bible, that they look back and see what must logically follow.

Arguments Against

with sin-lovers. I had planned to relate the revolting stories of two arch villains who would be comforted by this doctrine of truckling mercy, but a literary friend asks me to leave them out because they are too horrible to be believed. Suppose in their stead, I refer to the "sons of Belial" described in Judges 19 and ask if such men are any evidence of evolution, and if we should change the words of Jesus to read, "Blessed are the *unmerciful*: for they shall obtain mercy"? Could any mercy make *them* fit company for angels?

Be well advised that the people so generous with mercy that costs them nothing, have no notion of disturbing their own peace with fawning mercy. It requires only a mushy sentiment *to coddle crime and be prodigal with a mercy that involves other people's comfort and safety.* Ex-Gov. "Ma" Ferguson of Texas is said to have turned loose more than 3,000 criminals *to live neighbors to other people.* She is not likely to taint the exclusive circle of her presence with the menace of their society. *Let the common people be plagued with their rascality.* If there was a law that all pardoned criminals must live near the ones who pardoned them, there would be fewer pardons. It is so easy and seems so generous to pardon all hell into heaven, even if the man who plans it *would rather have a cur dog in his family than any one of half the poor people in his city.* Would it not distress these generous teachers who are so willing to fill heaven with "sons of Belial," if they had to live with them for eternity, or even keep them overnight?

The popular excuse offered for such doctrinal bushwhacking is that "Everyone has a right to his own opinion." Some people take it for granted that any sort of mental dugout of opinion confers an ownership and sacred immunity that even God is bound to respect.

Stop and think!

When an opinion is offered as a substitute for the revelation of God, *the man behind the opinion is thereby offered, to the same extent, as a substitute for God.* He who inhabits eternity does not submit his revelations to popular referendum nor to the veto of self-appraised scholarship. People who follow a man who *does not know*, rather than the God *who does know*, may find that they have gambled, with their souls at stake, and have *lost all they had that would hold mercy,* even if mercy deluged them.

Can mercy change the *memory* of one who has rotted his own soul, while infecting others, so that he can *remember* how saintly he was? Can God be honest and write into a man's eternity a false record of what he never was and never wished to be—a righteousness that he hated as much as he loved sin? There is only one way to escape the logic that "We must all appear before the judgment seat of Christ; that every one may receive the deeds done in his body"; that is to assume that God can say to the sinner who shrinks from the hell within himself, *"You are not yourself; you are someone else."* Milton makes one of his characters say, *"Myself am hell."*

If there is no limit to mercy, why make it depend on a gesture? Limitless mercy is unconditioned mercy, is it not? If there is some condition to mercy, then how could a well fed, tastily dressed, highly honored guesser, know what the conditions are? You are not safely guided by such a man unless he has a superior kind of a brain-pot that stews out an infallible brain-fog on which one may stake his soul.

Great wisdom and great folly may take turns in the same brain. Such folly is not easily seen if it is hidden in a fog of words or a wilderness of speculation. This eminent leader offers uneasy souls the comfort of his opinion and with two dozen words he presents a theory of time and eternity to be taken with one gulp. If he had stopped with "this world" the folly would have been apparent. If he had said, "I do not believe God will let people suffer for sin in the next world, because he does not allow it is this world," the nonsense of the statement would have been on the surface.

Not only do people suffer for their sins in this world, but they suffer for the sins of the race in ages past. The fact that an innocent child may suffer for the sins of its parents, witnesses that sin begets its own hell and sin in the *stream of life* becomes *penalty in the eddying pool.* Sin is more than some slight discourtesy to a whimsical God, to be cured with excuse-me-please mercy; it taints and warps the sinner and *begets a hatred for good.* All the poetical blarney about mercy that waits like a flunky for a beckoning hand, loses its charm when you hold it up against the tragedy of life.

A symbolical representation of the theory that God ordained that decillions of creatures should be fed into the slaughter mill as a part of the process that began with an amoeba and after 100,000,000 deaths evolved into a man. After man arrived, the mill kept on, but Jesus taught us to pray that God's Kingdom might come.

The truth sticks up like a rock in the froth and spume of human theories—GOD DOES LET THE WORLD SUFFER FOR THE SINS OF THE WORLD.

Far be it from me to deny that God answers prayer or that his mercy has any limitations other than what he has himself imposed. My contention is that it ill becomes a man to blame God for the cruelties of a billion years of supposed evolution and then hedge in his eternity with a limitless mercy that would make an angel out of a devil.

Does the same mouth blow hot and cold?

This sinner-soothing doctrine does not fit the facts of nature. There are some who profess to see God in nature. Such persons must know that there is nothing in nature that will dawdle and flirt and play the coquette with those who despise her laws. The man who breaks nature's laws needs to pray, *not to nature, but to a doctor*. Science may be able to baffle nature in some ways and parry the stroke of the avenger, but, left to itself, the stern old world maintains no mercy seat for belated wheedlers. If nature offers any prophecy of the judgment that awaits those who trifle with God, it is pronounced with four letters—d-o-o-m.

Note: When the type was set for this book, another page was needed to fill it out and I offer a catechism for children that seems to fit in here.

In the public press of Jan. 30, 1928, a column writer discusses a question of "Creative Evolution" and its "driving force" that is credited with having "evolved the amoeba into Plato." The versatile columnist says for the Christian, "He too 'sees God in gardens, forests, animals or mountain tops. . . .'" Certainly there is much in nature that, like a rainbow of promise, displays God's pledge that the World's hurt shall be cured (Isa. 11:6-9), but the man who can see God in the Juggernaut of creature struggle, ought to tremble in His presence. I cannot explain it to those whose brains are preempted to deny Eden, but some will understand. I give an imaginary conversation with a child.

Are bull-fights, dog-fights, cock-fights and such sports naughty?

Yes. The people who make creatures fight are put in jail (sometimes).

How can such fights in nature please God?

Arguments Against

My teacher says God plans such things to make amoebas into men.

Why does God keep it going after his men are made?

I will ask my teacher.

If men see God in all creatures, why do they spray fields, swamps and orchards with poison?

Maybe it is to help God kill more.

When a mammy cat gives a live mouse to her kittens to torture, can the mouse see that it is a divine arrangement?

My papa will not allow anything tortured.

What kind of little boys would stick poison needles in people and animals?

They would not be God's little boys.

Would they be God's little boys if they had wings like blood-sucking insects and could hum like mosquiotes?

Oh no! God wants little boys to be good.

If little boys killed mother birds and let the baby birds starve, like a hawk does, would God be pleased?

Their mammas would spank them and send them to bed without supper.

What would happen to little boys who pushed sharp hooks through little birds like owls do?

The Humane Society would put them in jail,

If the Humane Society could get what evolutionists call God, would they put Him in jail?

Oh no! They would go to heaven with Him.

(The author follows here the commonly accepted theory of heaven but does not vouch for it.)

Will everybody get to heaven?

Not unless God forgives them.

Must all people be forgiven before they can go to heaven?

Yes indeed.

How long does it take God to forgive people?

Only a minute.

How do people get to heaven?

The angels carry them.

How long does it take?

They get there the same day.

If it took God many millions of years to fight man's an-

The Gee-HAW of the Modern Jehu

cestors past trillions of foes and over mountains of bones *to get a man that is such a failure that he needs to be forgiven*, is it not a reversal of morals and methods and a panic of speed, to let the unfit survive, by forgiveness in one day and heaven in another?

Please ask my teacher.

Do animals need forgiveness?

Oh no! Animals do not sin.

Does evolution change animals that are fittest to survive, into men who are not fit to survive, so that God can forgive the unfitness and make the failures his own children?

It must be God's way.

What if the unfit men who have been made of the fittest animals and are then made fitter for heaven than animals, should sin after they get to heaven?

No one can sin in heaven.

Why not? Did not angels sin? If a billion years of evolution cannot make man sin-proof, fool-proof and failure-proof, how can one minute of heaven do it?

My teacher never told me that.

Would it not be better to believe that God made man in His own image, that man fell, and that God would restore the man to that likeness?

My teacher says that is not scientific.

Is heaven or forgiveness or the resurrection of Jesus scientific?

My teacher says science stops before it gets that far.

So it does but the pupils go right on to logical conclusions.

LOOK ABOUT YOU AND SEE.

Soliloquy: "We know that the whole creation groaneth and travaileth in pain together until now. . . . waiting. . . . "Rom. 8:22-23. Surely scholarship must be tipsy with the ferment of its own conceit when it hangs a halo of sanctity on the blood-lust of nature and undertakes to fit the steppings of God into the footprints of Satan.

Whatever else nature may reveal, it surely testifies that something has gone wrong with "all flesh," just as the book says. It is impossible to make a world of pillage and slaughter fit into the plan of a God who is good enough for heaven, unless something has happened that he is utterly displeased with. Will someone tell us why He taught us to pray, "Thy will be done on earth, as it is in heaven," if everything is

13

Arguments Against

evolving here according to his plan? One needs to be a lopsided poet to see beckoning love in a sunset and ignore the villainy of the mosquitoes. Long ago God said, "The earth also was corrupt before God and the earth was filled with violence." Even if it upsets all the theories of men who would make the stalking death of the jungle His plan for earth and the coddling of sin His plan for heaven, we may just as well recognize the truth that creature life is in a fever of struggle ending in a welter of death that others may live *and die.*

Since Jesus warned us that there would arise false Christs, it is only fair to ask concerning the God who is touted to be so indulgent: WHAT GOD?

Certainly not the God of the Bible.

Heb. 10:28 says, "He that despised Moses' law died without mercy ... Of how much sorer punishment, suppose ye, shall he be thought worthy, who hath trodden under foot the Son of God ... ?"

Of course, there are people who very cheerfully discredit anything in the Bible not to their liking, but people who call themselves Christians ought to accept the teachings of Jesus. Did he teach the endless, limitless forbearance of God?

He warned men of an unpardonable sin. Six times He describe the doom of the wicked as "weeping [or wailing] and gnashing of teeth." Matt. 23 records about forty epithets, accusations or words of doom that He used on some people of social and educational prominence. He asked one question that it takes a popular modern preacher to answer: "Ye serpents, ye generation of vipers, how can ye escape the damnation of hell [gehenna]?" He called some people dogs, wolves, swine, goats, serpents, bad fish, tares, spoiled salt, and He never hinted that lifting a claw or a hoof would make them what they were not. If God has any plan for admitting shut-out virgins, feeding the guest without a wedding garment, renewing rejected invitations, excusing wicked servants or giving murderous husbandmen another chance, Jesus kept it a secret. If the unmerciful can obtain mercy, the spoiled salt be resalted, the fixed gulf unfixed and God can be trifled with safely, Jesus had ample opportunity to tell us.

14

I would not leave the impression that anyone is finally shut out until he has silenced the wooing whisper of God in his heart. Indeed, I have no notion of making *any* program for God to follow, but I would warn any reader not to presume on gratuitous mercy of God beyond what his word warrants. I protest that I am not eager to have anyone damned. Not one child of God but would be glad to know that no soul will be so hopelessly warped that God must say, "Depart from me." If Jesus could have saved Jerusalem, He would not have wept over it and pronounced its doom. Before we veto the decrees of God, we ought to know, or be conceited enough to think we know, how He could do it better. If there are fountains of mercy that God has not told us about, I hope I shall be one to rejoice when they are revealed; on the other hand, it is cruelty limited only by eternity, to put a poultice on the festering sore of the world's sin when only a knife will cure. There are more than 31,000 verses in the Bible in which God could have told us that sin is only a delay or a detour on the way to glory. I find it impossible to believe that He has delegated the job of amending His revelations, to any brain stuff that reckons itself to be only six inches away from its "gill-slits."

It requires a sublime conceit to presume to do God's thinking for Him, but what adjectives will describe the arrogance that will *try to pass off the fog of a human brain for the afterthought of God or the thought of an after-God?*

I have been asked to explain what I mean by the expression, "the afterthought of God or the thought of an after-God." I mean that the God who would plan a help-yourself heaven for incorrigibles is so different from the God of the pitiless struggle of a theoretical evolution, that He must be a more recent God or He has had a more recent thought. Of course, I do not accept either theory.

When a man believes that he an amoeba plus a great many amendments, he is apt to show scant patience with any God that was good enough for mankind *before Darwin classified us.*

Any narcotic teaching that benumbs man's feeling that eternity will be the crop of his own sowing, will encourage sin. If one little gesture *after* death will change the harvest of a lifetime of "sowing to the flesh," then it will do more than human efforts can do *before* death. David sinned griev-

15

Arguments Against

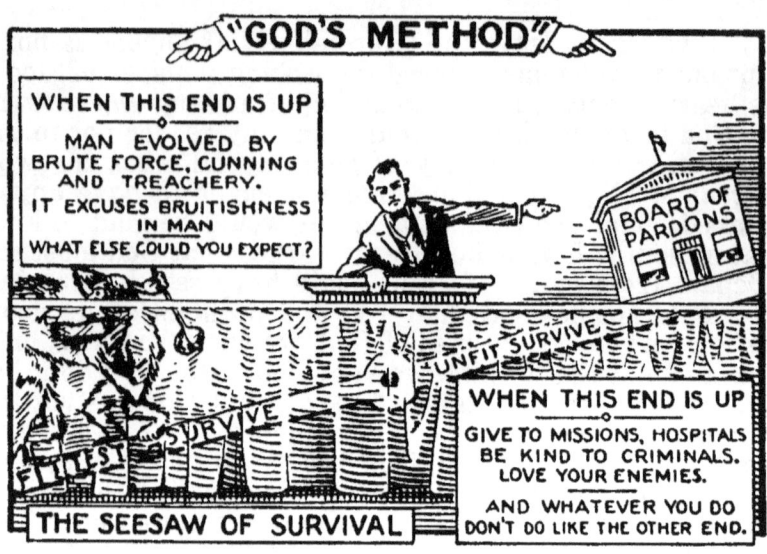

It takes 36 states to amend our federal Constitution and it puts a strain on one's credulity, to believe that any pod of brains that ripened on a limb next to the ape limb, can put the fundamentals of Almighty God on a teeter-board balanced with human theories.

Can you believe a Divine Father would use unnumbered ages of brute selfishness and cruelty, to change a docile amoeba into a savage man and then draft a missionary to save the savage and get him ready for heaven in a few hours. Ages of failure; success in a few hours.

17

ously and after a soul wracking repentance, found mercy, *but did not escape the harvest.* The prophet said to him, "The sword shall never depart from thine house," and shame, treachery and bereavement dogged his path until the end. If death brings cheaper mercy, why not wait for cut rates?

If mercy is unlimited, one need not cease from iniquity even in heaven. This would assume that when God said, "He that is filthy, let him be more filthy still," He meant that there would be nothing in a "modern" heaven to make a filth-lover uneasy, more than there is in the preaching of a "modern" gospel.

The dreadful tragedy of this gates-ajar doctrine is wrapped up in the supposition that *when one has trampled on mercy, all he needs is more mercy.* Many who trust in this false hope are blind to the fact that they have resisted mercy till it has warped and festered their souls and they hate what God loves and love what He hates. The scheme is based on crude shortsighted selfishness. It seeks only the comfort of the moral pervert and ignores the rights of God. It would provide endless mercy and eternal forbearance without changing facts that are everlastingly loathsome to God.

Eternity is not a question of what God will do with a naughty child; it turns on the finality of a choice that links one up with the friends or foes of God. There may be some *temporary* comfort in believing that sin is only the outcroppings of our brute ancestry; it may quiet one's fears of the wrath of God to believe that God is so committed to mercy that he cannot help himself, but—

"THE DEVILS BELIEVE AND TREMBLE."

LATEST STYLES IN CREED

I have lived longer than Methuselah, if life be measured not by the revolutions of the earth but those of society and philosophy. The latest "trend of thought" is about as permanent as hoop skirts. ANYTHING FOR A CHANGE.

When I broke with freethinkers and Darwinism, the church was so careful to make the cure complete that they stood me up six times to pledge allegiance to the faith "ONCE FOR ALL DELIVERED." Now I have lived to see my outcasts come in the front door of the church and berate me bacuse I do not REINTERPRET my vows.

In those days the creation story was considered either history or hoax; sacred truth or a hoary headed lie. Now, the reigning styles in "new conception" infer that it started somewhere as a lie and, like a persimmon, improves with age. After many centuries, it is now sacred folklore and tradition. God could have corrected it any time but He let it go as about THE BEST HE COULD DO for a people so RECENTLY CREATED IN HIS IMAGE.

Later on, according to high salaried men, Mary lied to the angel or the angel lied to Mary, or the Bible lies about both (Luke 1:34-35) and the tale of a Virgin birth got started. While God was inspiring ANY of the BIBLE He could have corrected this, but the church was not far enough from Pentecost and needed a miracle yarn to enable them to compete with other half baked religions.

In th days of Ingersoll, the church believed that God was grieved that "all flesh had corrupted his way," as Genesis 6:12 says. Now, one of the few theories that Bible-repair men can agree on, is that a protracted carnival of horrors that they call evolution, was the delight of whoever, whatever, however God is, and that He gave prizes of survival and mates to the best killers and made them His proxies in refining the mud to make a man.

If Ingrsoll had lived now, he would find many that Jesus said would come in His name, such congenial imitators, that, like Darrow and Lindsey, he would be forced to resurrect some new adomination of heathenism *in order to keep ahead* of his brethren of more pius phrases, who hanker to head some pilgrimage to some new deliverance.

19

Once there was a boy who thought "Doctor of Divinity" meant one who gives treatments to Divinity—perhaps surgery and grafting. Later, he learned that many D. D.'s are humble servants of the Great Physician who healed *with* Divinity. What does the word mean in your community?

DR. CADMAN APOLOGIZES FOR THE BIBLE

Someone has written this learned man about the capture of Jericho by Israel and asks, "Does a just Deity ever injure one nation for the good of another?"

I quote some sentences from the doctor's reply that appeared in the public press Oct. 19, 1927. "God often appears in an unfavorable light in Old Testament narratives because its earlier writers persisted in attributing to him deeds which were entirely man's." "According to their point of view, Jehovah commanded the capture of Jericho; according to ours, He did not." "The God Christ revealed had to slowly educate the nations to His standards." "He is not the tribal Deity of outworn conception, but the universal Father of present knowledge."

In these fastidious days there are many eminent people trying to fix up the reputation of God so that He can go in fashionable society. They fear that people interested in prize-fights, murder trials and the destruction of potential life might be shocked at Scripture severities.

Many students of history understand that God has blessed the nations that believed the Bible and visited His displeasure on those who nullified any part that interfered with their opinions. Jesus said, "YE DO ERR, NOT KNOWING THE SCRIPTURES." Now we have men in intellectual authority and *many thousands of echo-men* who say, *"Ye do err, not knowing BETTER than the Scriptures."*

Most of them are too cautious to say it out boldly, that Jesus is a back number; that will hardly be a popular apology in most churches, until the public is educated up to it.

If Joshua was deceived in supposing God had commissioned him to destroy Jericho, then of course Moses was deceived in supposing God kept him busy for forty years getting ready for it and Abraham was deceived in believing God had deeded this land to Abraham's children. If it was all a mistake, then Stephen was deceived in believing that God drove out these nations before Israel (Acts 7:45).

Psalms 103:7, says "He made known his ways unto Moses." Isaiah 63:12 says that God "led them by the right hand of Moses." Jesus said, "The Scribes and Pharisees sit in Moses' seat: all therefore whatsoever they bid you observe, that observe and do." Also, "Had ye believed Moses, ye would have believed me." The New Testament testifies that Moses came from the unseen world to commune with Jesus about the program of God (Luke 9:31). If Dr. Cadman's apology is good, then much of the Bible is not good and the next logical step will be to apologize for Jesus as having an "outworn conception."

If the Old Testament puts God "in an unfavorable light," then *this honored churchman puts Him in a worse*. If the Old Testament *is* the Word of God, it puts some prominent people in unfavorable light.

One way to show the folly that lurks in such a question and answer, is to ask it in an amended form. Let me try it?

Does a just Deity ever preserve strict neutrality while one nation is injured for the good of another?

Jericho was destroyed.

"Modernists' do not overwork their Deity with miracles and such things and they cannot presume that He was too far behind with His work to concern Himself with this battle. Was He unable to interfere? Would not neutrality discredit Him more than to foster "the survival of the fittest"? Would not a God who supervised the killing of the weak by the strong (if evolution is God's method) be bored with too much peace? Why not? Seeing Dr. Cadman is an evolutionist, it may be pertinent to ask if a God who delighted in the slaughter of multiplied billions every second of the day of every year for a million ages, would be squeamish about the overthrow of a nation of *unspeakable nastiness* by a nation that stood for decency?

Though I believe God could not be entertained with the needless horrors of a system that would evolve a fish *out of the sea* to struggle for existence on the land and after ages of hardship, evolve it *back into the sea* as a whale, or the scheme that would evolve a horse out of an insect eating reptile and then evolve stinging flies to torture it; I do believe that a sin-hating God would be as likely to dispossess a depraved nation as a farmer is likely to clear a field of briars when he wishes more wheat and fewer thorns. I can easily believe that a kind hearted farmer might decide to have more chickens and fewer weasels.

The doctor explains that God "had to slowly educate the nations to his standards." Well, it appears that *about the time he finishes the education of a nation, it is dead.* I quite agree that God *does* try to teach living nations with the object lessons of dead ones and it *is* a slow process.

If this is not God's method of educating the nations, then one wonders WHO IS TEACHING THE SCHOOL THAT MAKES BERTHS FOR THE BATS AND BANQUETS FOR BUZZARDS?

Dr. Cadman's "point of view" seems to be that during the 4,000 years of Old Testament history God could not make his dear children understand that they were killing his dear children. This is evident from his remark that "He loves all men and all are His children." It argues that He is not a fortunate Father in having such stupid children, so utterly unlike Him that for 40 centuries either He could not make Himself heard or the children understood Him to mean exactly the opposite from what He taught them.

If a human father had sons who understood everything he said, to mean exactly the opposite, would he not, after a while, decide to stop talking or tell them *not to do* what he *wished them to do?* Dare we presume that Dr. Cadman's "point of view" is that God could have told Joshua to kill and Joshua understanding the orders to mean the opposite, as usual, would have stopped the killing, or are we to suppose that God could not or did not speak Joshua's' language?

Will someone show me the way out of the fog?

What kind of general would it be who would let his armies fight 4000 years because every time he *thought* they ought to retreat, they *imagined* he wished them to charge?

It might be an evolutionary general who had loved combat for a hundred million years and being tongue-tied his soldiers did not know he had changed his mind.

If Old Testament writers put God in an "unfavorable light," what kind of light do modern luminaries put Him in?

One needs to be under-witted or water-logged with profundity, to believe that God would work with His dirt a hundred million years, mixing and remixing, sifting and resifting, skimming and reskimming *to make a man that He cannot talk to and be understood.*

If God succeeds, after a while, in educating the fight out of man, when will He begin on the brutes and how soon will the mites of the "seven-year" itch learn that they were designed to promote sleep? From the conditions in the world today, it would seem we are *"getting no better fast."* The utter failure of the educational "viewpoint" needs no better testimony than the words of Dr. Cadman himself in the public press Jan. 18, 1928. Speaking of the French Revolution he said, "The naked realism of an obsession for 'liberty' took possession of them and drove them far below the levels of the brute ... The lesson is that human nature has in it vile potentialities which some of its eulogists ignore. These potentialities emerge in chaotic moments when the restraints of law and order are thrown off."

Where would human nature get "vile potentialities" to enable men to go "far below the level of the brute"? Jesus gave us the answer. He said to the devil's children, "Ye do the deeds of your father." Really, it is easier to believe that man fell as the Book says, and that he did not fall UP. The world needs SALVATION more than it needs EDUCATION.

Fundamentalists are eager to admit that God's will is often misunderstood and defied by wayward men. Certainly men have thought they were doing God's will when they were doing the opposite, because *sin has blinded spiritual eyes, deafened spiritual ears and warped the thinking of the nations.*

Dr. Cadman flounders in the same tangle that has snared every Bible expositor who tries to formulate a consistent theology on the theory that all men are the children of God. Jesus knew better. He said to some, "I know that ye are Abraham's seed ... If ye were Abraham's children, ye would do the works of Abraham ... If God were your Father, ye would love me ... Ye are of your father the devil, and the lusts of your father ye will do" (John 8:37-44). In Matt. 13:38, He contrasts "the children of the kingdom" and "the children of the wicked one." In that wonderful prayer before He entered Gethsemane, He said, "I pray for them [disciples]: I pray not for the world, but for them which thou hast given me; for they are thine."

This will not convince anyone who nullifies every Scripture not to his notion. Men who wear out Scriptural conceptions of God are not likely to say, "This verse does not agree with me, but I believe it."

The Gee-HAW of the Modern Jehu

If I cannot convince Theistic-Evolutionists that their double-barreled name shoots in opposite directions, perhaps some farmer's boy can explain it to them. I offer a lesson in the form of question and answer that only a clever man can befog with words.

LESSON FOR BEGINNERS

Children, how do poultry men develop a laying strain of hens?

By selecting the best layers to breed from.

How do they develop a fighting strain of chickens?

By selecting the best fighters to breed from.

In a fighting world, what is meant by "survival of the fittest"?

The survival of the fighting-est.

If, for a hundred million years, God was pleased to give survival to the best fighters and the ones that looked out for themselves, what would it indicate?

That such a God wanted fighters and self-seekers.

Since man is the supposed masterpiece of a supposed evolution that is supposed to have taken many millions of years to breed a man by a supposed survival of the fittest, how shall we arrive at super-man level?

By killing off pacifists, weaklings and unselfish people.

—o—

25

Arguments Against

Perhaps some reader will demur to this with the suggestion that survival depended also upon speed and ability to hide. Certainly, but even pigeons and rabbits settle their matings and tenant rights by combat. When weaker creatures all escape from a fox, they really kill him with starvation, do they not? Is there anything unselfish in a rabbit running away from a fox and leaving the hungry brute to feast on a whole nest of partridges?

One wonders just what Israel could have done to fit into the new "viewpoint." They could have gone back to Egyptian slavery or perished in the desert. They might have merged with the Canaanites and participated in the unprintable deviltry of heathen worship—as some of them did. The modern "viewpoint" has been unable to prevent the world's greatest slaughter-fest, but it is easy to sit in an armchair and indulge one's leadership, like a child directing the animals into a toy "Noah's ark," *improving on Noah's arrangement.*

There is no evidence that God filed a protest before Jericho was destroyed or rebuked the victors after it happened. Though God had scores of prophets—men willing to die for the truths they proclaimed—not one of them ever repudiated the "viewpoint" of Joshua. Jesus whose name was the New Testament form of "Joshua"—Jesus the descendant of the woman who betrayed Jericho—evidently had the same "viewpoint," for He never offered any apology for the unpleasantness that the Canaanites or any other degenerates suffered, but *He promised more trouble to more sinners than any man who ever lived.*

As for "tribal Deity," it pleased God to reveal Himself to later nations through the Hebrews. Jesus said, "Salvation is of the Jews," also, He said in the presence of a Canaanitish woman, "I am not sent but unto the lost sheep of the house of Israel." Fundamentalists are children of Abraham by faith.

The expression, "outworn conception," indicates that conceptions wear out and by the same token, the doctor's conception must go sooner or later, *depending on how many have used it before him.* If this is true, I am comforted with the reflection that my Old Testament conception wears

The Gee-HAW of the Modern Jehu

out only a little while before his and *future generations will pity the ignorance of both.* However, I fear *we stake our souls upon our conceptions* for it is not at all clear to me that when "the great day of His wrath is come," God will send the "outworn conceptions" to hell and the worn-out conception incubators to heaven. If I wrap my soul in conceptions that wear out, I fear my rags will go with me where I go. If I believe as much and nullify as little of the Holy Scriptures as Jesus did (I believe He accepted all), I shall be in good company. *God will not upbraid me for believing the Bible TOO MUCH.*

If Dr. Cadman spanks with one hand and pats with the other, the pats are worse than the spanks. After putting God in an "unfavorable light," he offers Him the compliment of "universal Father of present knowledge."

What present knowledge?

Could it be the knowledge of T. N. T., poison gas, bombing planes, submarines, habit-forming drugs and prophylactics?

Since the major portion of eminent scientists have rejected the "viewpoint" and the not-yet-worn-out conception of Dr. Cadman, we may well ask if it is the "present knowledge" that manifests itself in the propaganda for atheism, goat marriage, behaviorism, prenatal destruction of life, monkey-grafting, displays of nakedness, smutty books and plays, or perhaps the knowledge of how to live without work and not be bored.

Could it be the knowledge that has lifted our nation to where 50,000,000 people listen in on a prize fight that in newspaper space, time given and money lost, would keep every needy orphan on earth in school for a year?

Is it the knowledge that stimulated the students of a great university to celebrate a football victory by mauling the police and burning school buildings?

There is a march of world events that moves great statesmen to warn us that another world war will destroy civilization. But for the mercy of God, this is true, *but it is not new knowledge.* IF THE PROPHECIES OF JESUS WERE PROTECTED BY COPYRIGHT, SUCH STATESMEN COULD BE PROSECUTED. See Matt. 24:21.

Arguments Against

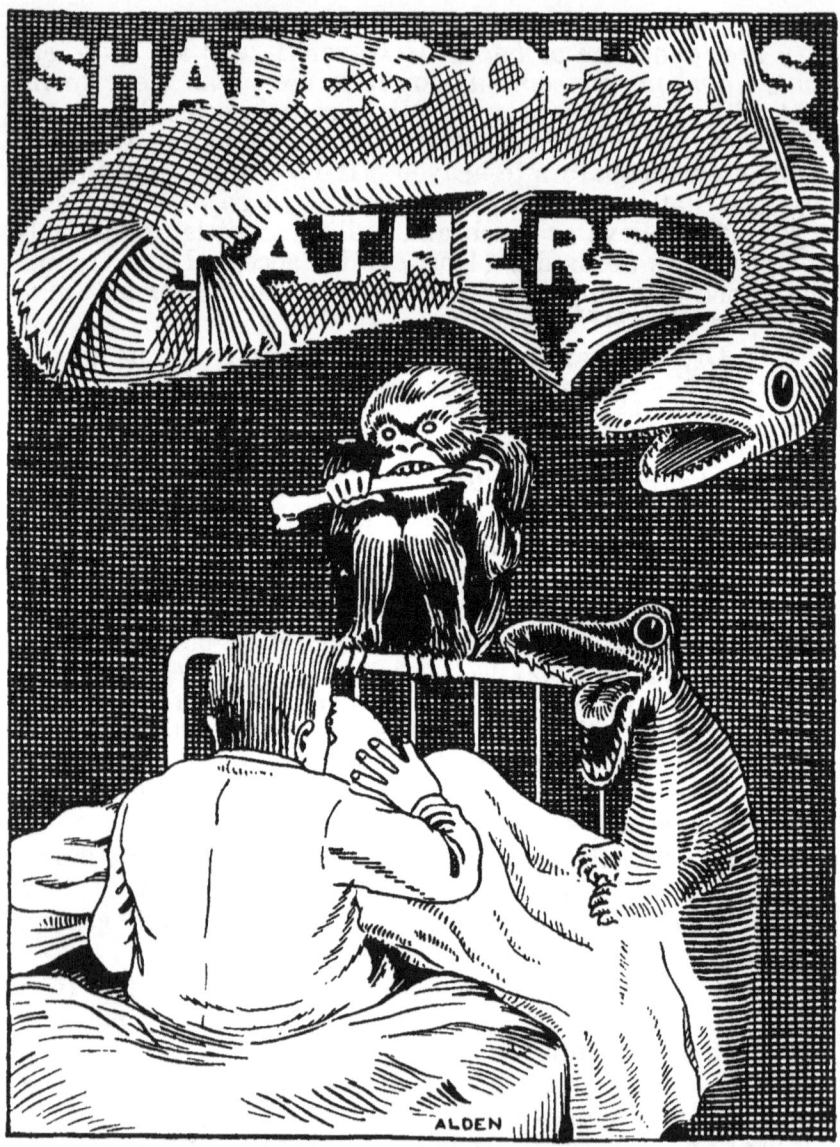

Go back to the school room and inspire little children! You make a good cloak for sin but you are poor company in a bed room.

Ancestor architects disagree as to some items, but these figures approximate in outline—if not in size—the 'pithecus, reptile and fish that some of them have put in our pedigree.

Even if the ghosts of our alleged REPTILE ancestors came back to crawl on our beds and force us to own them with a good night kiss, not even that could give us a conception of a better educated or more indulgent God.

When the doctor says, "The God Christ revealed had to slowly educate the nations to His standards," I am moved to ask as humbly as I may,

WHAT ARE HIS STANDARDS?

WHAT STANDARDS IS HE EDUCATING THEM AWAY FROM?

If man has been evolving UPWARD for hundreds of millions of years, where did he get the standards that need to be reversed? The amoeba is a very gentle creature; who educated into it a standard that needs to be educated out? Will it take as long to educate it out as it did to educate it in?

What different God did Christ reveal?

Jesus (the New Testament name for Joshua) said, "Woe unto thee Chorazin! . . . Bethsaida! . . . And thou, Capernaum, which art exalted unto heaven, shalt be brought down to hell [hades] . . . it shall be more tolerable for the land of Sodom in the day of judgment than for thee." (Matt. 11:21-44.)

Of Jerusalem, he said, "Thine enemies . . . shall lay thee even with the ground . . . and they shall not leave in thee one stone upon another; because thou knewest not the time of thy visitation." (Luke 19:43-44.)

Speaking of reckoning day, he said, "But those mine enemies, which would not that I should reign over them, bring hither, and slay them before me." (Luke 19:27.)

To Pilate He said, "If my kingdom were of this world, then would my servants fight . . ." Now read the last three verses of Joshua 5th and decide for yourself whether or not the Field Marshal of Jehovah directed the battle of Jericho.

If there lingers in the mind of the reader any fancy that Jesus abandoned the "outworn conception" that "modernists" have worn out, once more I call attention to His words, when He spoke of the doom of the nations in the days of Noah, "Even thus shall it be in the day when the Son of man is revealed." (Luke 17:30.)

Any dallying process that is relied upon to "slowly educate the nations," must be working in reverse; if the Bible does not reveal this, the newspapers do. The folly of such philosophy may be illustrated by

A PARABLE OF FOLLY

Once there was a woman who loved cats and birds.

She pitied all cats that were sick, deserted, forlorn.

From the alleys of a great city, she gathered homeless cats and gave them a home with the colored cook on her park-like estate.

This same woman was much distressed with cat fights, but the cats disregarded her lectures. Many kittens were born on this cat ranch and were promptly destroyed by uneducated Toms. Many birds nested in the trees and bushes and many baby birds went to fatten the cats. All this added to the yearnings of the governess of cats.

(Thus far, the parable is based on actual facts; what follows is fiction.)

Being a lover of both cats and birds, she decided that cat morals would respond to a slow process of education, believing that if the cats were allowed to fight and eat birds they would, after many thousands of years, come to love each other, eat grass and dig worms for the birds.

EVEN GREAT MEN WITH ELASTIC DEFINITIONS AND HYPNOTIC ELOQUENCE CANNOT RECONCILE A CAT-FIGHT PAST WITH A DOVE-LOVE FUTURE AS THE WHIM OF A CHANGEABLE GOD.

THE FOOLISHNESS OF GOD

Some months ago, I attended a meeting without my glasses and asked the Bible students present to help me quote a verse of Scripture. I told them it was something about the foolishness of God or man and would be something near one of four statements:

"The foolishness of God is wiser than men."

"The wisdom of men is foolishness with God."

"The foolishness of man is wiser than God."

"The wisdom of God is foolishness with men."

It was unanimously agreed that I was trying to quote I. Cor. 3:19 and there was much surprise when I asked them to read I Cor. 1:25. It seemed unthinkable that the Bible would speak of the foolishness of God.

Call it irony, hyperbole or covert sarcasm, yet it is evident that there are no words in human language to adequately express God's contempt for any bowl of brains that appoints itself a kind of Board of Review to pass upon the conduct of God.

If the Word had said that only one in ten thousand could hopefully weigh their wisdom against the foolishness of God, every cult and college and newspaper might furnish a candidate, but it made no provision for any man to do God's thinking for Him. It must mean that if I were a double-witted man, I could not qualify as a half-wit in the parliament of God. If God needs an apology or a new revelation of Himself, let Him make it.

How rich we are in having a God so great that a thinking level that would be foolishness for Him, is so far above man's strutting conceit that no brain-brewed philosophy can reach high enough "to touch bottom." The A B C of wisdom is to realize that an infinite God might do many things that a finite mind would not approve of. It is a good preventative of mental auto-intoxication, to remind ourselves that *what we think we would have done, if God had left it to our judgment, cannot determine what God might have done before we arrived.*

31

Any one of these books will be sent for 20c. No extra charge to foreign countries unless the rates shall change.

With every dollar order we will give two or more 8 page pamphlets free, as, "When Snakes Began to Nurse their Young" — the author's reply to Brisbane, and "One Hundred Questions for Teachers of Evolution."

After you have ordered a book, we will send you 10 books of that kind at half price. You may loan them, give them away or sell them. We do not mix books to make up the 10. Lower prices for 100.

For $5.00, we will mail 50 books — any that you select — to as many as 50 addresses that you furnish. This means that 50 people get one book, or 25 get two each, or as you direct.

Unless otherwise stated, all books postpaid.

HOMO PUBLISHING CO.
Rogers, Ohio

Arguments Against

Arguments Against

Since Mother Eve listened to the first Word-loosener, it has been the work of Satan and some who will run his errands, to tone down, reinterpret and explain away the warnings of God and unscare those who have reason to fear "the great day of His wrath."

Copyright 1928 by B. H. Shadduck

Arguments Against

WHAT IT IS ALL ABOUT

There is testimony in dust. (Mark 6:11).

In the charnal heaps of the past, God has written for the present.

"History repeats itself." Its tragic scenes must be reenacted because man has not learned WHY. It would be a wise nation indeed, that was fully warned by the wreckage of others.

Men who reject those parts of the Bible that proclaim the doomsdays of an offended God, have yet to explain *the same kind of record, written larger in the tumbled walls of a thousand buried cities.* If the Bible does not fit your notion of God, where was *your* God when great nations collapsed?

Where was the modernist's God when, on proud Babylon's palace wall, a ghostly hand wrote for an insulting king and his flunkies, the doom of a kingdom? If you doubt the reality of that hand, the ruins spell out the same message.

Nineteen hundred years ago the hated Nazarene wrote in the Jerusalem dust a writing soon shuffled out by the feet of the heedless throng. Perhaps it was the same decree that was written in the dust with falling tears when He gave the city over to its fate. Perhaps He wrote in the dust what was, in a few years, *written large enough for the world to read,* by the Roman legions.

When He went the way to Calvary, he turned once, long enough to pronounce the doom of a nation. Silent before the high priest, (Matt. 26:63), silent before Herod (Luke 23:9), silent before Pilate (Matt. 27:12,14), Jesus —the sport of the rabble—turned all blood-wet and uttered words that later found echo in the rhythm of marching armies.. If there are some who doubt the Bible record, *nineteen centuries have not effaced the conditions He foretold.*

In this book I would not mock at scholarship. *We know too little.*

We are dreadfully informed in ways that cannot save us and woefully ignorant of danger. There never was a time when the world had so many encyclopedias in book covers and under hats, yet with all our doctors (D.D., L.L.D., Ph. D.) the world is alarmingly sick. Our schools would dwarf the ancient temple; so would our prisons. We are so bulging with information that it is now possible for one man above the clouds, to destroy a city in 30 minutes.

Jerusalem was headquarters for knowing ones who were blind on the God side (Luke 19:42, 44). Deny the words of Jesus, but you cannot deny the fulfillment. Sometimes the buzzards are tutors, and the world has not yet graduated from the school of ruins.

Am I pessimistic?

Not unless my mind is wandering.

I know that men have prepared many resignations for Jehovah and have thrust oft repeated farewells upon Him, but I have the comforting conviction that He has not gone anywhere. The God who put a Paradise at both ends of the Bible will make good every prophecy that lies between.

2

ALIBI, LULLABY, BY-BY

(Authorities differ in spelling by-by; we use the shorter form.)
By B. H. SHADDUCK, PH. D.

Alibi?

Let the witty colored man explain it.

"Alibi is when the lawyer prove you *is* where you *ain't* so the jury specify you *ain't* where you *is* when you *was*. After the co't house adjourn, the lawyer man say, 'Client, you is cleared; you is scientifically not guilty, but promise me you is more cautious enough in the future'."

This is the picture in miniature of man's age-long eagerness to accept any two-faced theory that winks one way at sin and another way at reform.

I have known a man to strut his pedigree and expect the homage of common people as a tribute properly due to one having his proud family name. I have known the same man to excuse his sins and promise himself easy mercy after death, on the plea that *God cannot expect chastity from sensual humans so recently descended from the ancestors of apes.* The sin-lover finds it very consoling to meditate on how well he is doing considering the fact that his ancestry was 99.9% brute, but you start a fight if you suggest a lowly pedigree when he parades his social prominence.

This brute beginning is very convenient as an alibi for sin and a starting point from which to measure a very flattering progress, but *keep it far enough in the past not to monkeyfy our caste.* I have seen somewhere the intellectual offering of some theorist that some races evolved from a lower type of animal, or at least more recently. It will help to escape the evidence of human depravity, if they will fix up a sliding scale of remoteness. Some wealthy people who seek a basis for nobility would pay well to be rated among those who began to be cannibals 2,000,000 years before the riff-raff.

You may have observed that a man on trial for murder, having no other defense, will hire scientists to swear that he was mentally unbalanced and that insanity runs in the family, but do not twit him of it after he is acquitted. For the same reason men with a conviction for sin, find relief in believing the God who stewed His material in a billion years of brutality before He fashioned it into a man, cannot be

3

much displeased when He finds the product soggy with broth. If bestiality runs in the fish-reptile-man family by the will of God, how can such a God suddenly change His mind and expect heaven fruit on a limb fed with monkey sap?

I know, of course, that men seldom give to themselves a reason for their mental attitudes and few evolutionists know why they are so eager to prove their theory, but down in the sub-cellar of man's moral consciousness there lurks a willingness to discredit anything that discredits him. Here is a sample of such a hankering for monkey kinship that amounts almost to a passion.

On the front page of the Pittsburgh Chronicle Telegraph dated Sept. 30, 1926, there is a column written by one of our modern oracles who is equipped with such a diversified line of wares that he is a kind of intellectual Sears and Roebuck. He says, "Prof. Heberlein, excavating in Java, has discovered a complete skull of the prehistoric ape-like creature known as the Pithecanthropus Erectus, the 'missing link' between apes and man." Let the reader consider well the words "known as." *They have a name for it before they find it. After making images and pictures of a theoretical creature and calling it "science," they comb the earth to find a bone that can be guessed into the supposition.* Continuing, he says, "It is to be hoped that Professor Heberlein will hurry home with his find. If the evidence that man and the ape had the same great great grandparents is now beyond dispute, bonfires should be built throughout the civilized world."

What is the hurry?

Why the hilarity? What shall we gain? From whence comes this craving to rob the ape of his exclusiveness and break into his pedigree? I think I know.

Do not deceive yourself by supposing that it is the ape's pedigree that they are so eager to share; it is the ape's escape from judgment that they covet. It is not so much where man came from as it is *where he is going*, that disturbs sinners. *The front end of the Bible is not so offensive to the "modernist" as the last end.* If God did not create man from the dust, He will not raise him from the dust (Dan. 12:2). Comparatively few men read with comfort of a "white throne" and opening books on the reckoning day

4

of God, and it will comfort many, if the first three chapters of the Book can be so emptied of meaning that the last three will upset with lopsidedness.

This does not apply to all evolutionists. Many have never thought it out; many accept the theory because it is reckoned to be a mark of intellectuality and many students have accepted evolution because it has been dinned into them at taxpayers' expense and claims "the weight of scholarship." "The weight of scholarship" is always on the side of the ones who hold the scales and *agnostics and atheists are beginning to hold some of the scales.*

Certainly I do not mean to say that the avowed purpose of *all* who deny Bible statements, is to excuse human depravity or assure themselves against a "day of wrath," but I do say that this is the logical outcome of the movement and *the results are already on display.* If I were a lunatic and could have five minutes of sanity, it would take only four to reason it out that to discredit the Bible, must loosen the moral restraints of the nation. *Thinking people will not long be satisfied with a doubtful Bible nor with a half-breed religion that is a cross between a happen-so menagerie and a hope-so heaven.* If man is better now than Adam, it needs no bloody cross to restore him to a God-likeness from which he never fell. *If man fell UP and is yet falling UP, there is nothing for God to do but keep out of the way, and that is exactly what ultra "modernists" want him to do.* If this statement seems too strong, I offer a sample of such conceit. I have on my table as I write, a paper called American Farming, dated February, 1926, and *claiming* a circulation of 700,000. Among the advertisements, I notice pictures of 19 pistols and 2 stills, also an offer of free "liberal" literature and some other literature that is "Daringly Different." On page 26, there is a signed article by a pastor at Cowden, Ill. I do not give his name; he may have a family. I quote just two sentences. *"Some folks are standing today where God was a century ago wondering why He is not with them. He has moved on, expecting us to follow."* There is a note of self-abasement in this, for he concedes the point that *as late as February, 1926, God was somewhere in front.*

5

Arguments Against

(By Courtesy of Houghton Mifflin Company)

HEAVEN A DREAM

Here is evidence that 100% "modernists" **are consistent** enough to deny the Garden of God at *both ends of the Bible*. This picture of Darwin appears in a periodical that calls itself The Christian Century (I do not know what God calls it). This publication refused to advertise the Jocko-Homo series of books, but it did advertise this avowedly anti-Christian book. You will note that the advertisement says of Darwin, "HE MADE HELL A LAUGHING STOCK AND HEAVEN A DREAM." More than this, "he upheaved the very foundations of religion and morality."

Is that what evolution does?

Yes. It does all that for people who accept it and follow it to a logical conclusion, but why The Christian Century advertises that fact and calls itself "Christian" though it refuses to advertise books that defend the Bible, is beyond my comprehension, unless it is to fulfill the words of Jesus, "Many shall come in my name."

If Mr. Darwin's theories could be demonstrated as facts and we could be sure that God could not or did not create one man and one woman, then it were better for humanity never to find it out. If we could know that life passed through trillions of loathsome bodies to come to us and if our brute ancestors buried side by side would make a field of bones reaching to the moon and the miseries they suffered would overwhelm the most literal hell, what good could come of teaching it to little children? If it were true and some man discovered our shame that God had kept covered for 6,000 years, he would be justified in saying, "I thought I bore the image of God, marred with sin, but I am nothing but *the warmed over leavings* of a billion generations of slimy crawling creeping climbing beasts and *if God will keep it from my children, I will.*"

Yet these ape-kin zealots will "compass land and sea" to convince the youth of the world that *the apes are several hundred million years nearer to man in the matter of creation than is God.* They say with a fine show of heroism that would almost convince one that they believe it, that science will be strangled if they are not permitted to teach little children that *they are the spawn of reptiles much refined by many hatchings.* They quote Jesus as though they were in league with Him, "The truth shall make you free." Free from what? Will this theory of evolution free the sinner from his sins? One is left to wonder how much greater the great saints and statesmen and reformers would have been

7

THE INDEPENDENT THINKER

Liberty is a word to conjure by. It is the rallying cry of heroes and demagogues. From truant school boy to anarchist, evil as well as good, clamor for freedom. Used as a battle cry against man's real foes, it may move all heaven to "amens," but as a declaration of independence from Divine restraint and warning, it amounts to nothing more than the bombast of a slave.

8

if they could have been free from the notion of God-kinship. How much greater would the old prophets have been if they could have known about their "gill-slits"?

THE UNFAIRNESS OF IT

Evolutionists plead for liberty to think.

Who has ever tried to cramp their thinking?

So far as I know, all the members of the Eden caste agree that if anyone wishes to put reptiles in his pedigree, he ought to be humored here or hereafter.

If I have ever denied their right to animal kinship, I apologize.

When I published "Puddle to Paradise," I asked the artist to make a composite picture of the ancestors they claim, and my information is that they do not like it. They argue for a frog-pond origin but resent any acceptance of the theory as applying to them.

Is freedom to be only for evolutionists? Will they accord us liberty to believe that we track back to God without going through a reptile wallow? Is there a greater crime against liberty than to compel Bible-believing parents to send their children to school and pay taxes to have their faith destroyed? Why are they not content to choose their own limb in the monkey tree and let us roost on another bush? *Because evolution would crawl into its hole and die if it were generally accepted that ONLY its devotees are the upper end of a fish-reptile-marsupial-whatnot succession.* They are happy in the contemplation of a kinship of belly-crawlers, only *if they can daub us with the same smear.*

I hope never to say as mean things about them as they have said about their ancestors.

A CHALLENGE

If liberty will die and science be strangled unless little children are taught that their pedigree came over from mud-puppy to an opossum-like animal in a bug-eating lizard (or some other combination), why not tell the whole brutal truth? Why keep the abysmal horrors of the theory hidden until the pupil has lost the direction of God? If present con-

JOCKO-HOMO'S LADDER

In the twenty years that Jacob toiled for Laban alone among the flocks, scorched with heat by day and chilled with frost by night, he was cheered with the memory of the night when he lay at the foot of the ladder of God — the pathway of angels.

Here is another kind of dream-ladder; more popular than it is inpiring. The artist had not room for all the rungs; the reader can supply many.

10

ditions on earth are the result of evolution instead of the corruption described in Genesis 6:12, then here is an unveiled lesson for beginners.

DO MEN GATHER GRAPES FROM THORNS?

The blood it has shed would make a river brimming the gorge of Niagara.

If every life it has taken could have a grain of sand dropped on the earth as a tombstone sent from the stars, we should be buried under a desert of sand 100 miles deep.

If every pain and pang it has caused could be wept over, it would take the hurricanes of the ages for sobs and drain the oceans for tears.

In describing the early home, H. G. Wells (evolutionist) says the children knocked the old man in the head when they were old enough.

And why not?

Isn't that exactly how undiluted evolution would behave?

Arthur Brisbane says, "Less than 50,000 years ago all human beings were cannibals except the lowest, most miserable specimens, too dull to kill anybody." Then we must have descended from the dull ones. Well, if we are to have evolution taught, let us have the whole brutal truth.

The logically alert evolutionists have found no place in the system for a compassionate God and *many of them find no need for any kind of God if they can only have an amoeba to start with.* The Humane Society would jail any man who entertained himself with the cruelties of evolution.

If God has been pleased with the way the world has been going, the devil might just as well resign. So far was Jesus from blaming either God or evolution for world conditions, that he called the evil one "the prince of this world," even as Paul called him, "the god of this world."

Evolution is presented to beginners as though it were some benevolent kind of process; as though an oyster is millions of years better off than an amoeba and a rabbit is much happier than a toad. They do not stress the point that a louse has an easier life than an elephant and that a stinging fly has the advantage of a horse. It seems to be the pol-

11

icy of teachers to omit the odious details until the pupils are inoculated. There are some who credit the sorry mess to God and *think they pay him a compliment.*

While the captains of this drive are willing to weaken the authority of the Bible, most of them are willing to crossbreed evolution with any kind of religion and raise ethical maxims to save civilization. When "flaming youth" is loosed from the restraint of a wholesome fear of God, he is not likely to bow his head to a halter of ideals. Ideals are not in great demand. You can go where young men congregate and sell a basket of bull pups before you can give away one high ideal. Keen minded youth will not be slow to discover that *evolution was never based upon morals, but worked best when its favorites obeyed the driving impulses of the flesh.*

When youth loses faith in the religion of the fathers, what is there to hold them to the moral standards of the fathers?

If evolution worked because lives as numberless as star dust were sacrificed and the winners were the ones that were brutishly alert, on what ground may an evolutionist rebuke brute standards in man?

Theistic evolution is an expression that, in its working clothes, means a divinely supervised breeding of reptiles and their ancestors and progeny, to arrive at man. Great evolutionists smile at the conceit but do not resent any faith in any God, *if He will keep up.* They are really generous to any church that is a camp-following church and will tag along in the wake of whatever passes for science. They even find the Bible convenient for mottoes and sentiments and enough moral doctrines to *flavor and filter evolutionism* so that its brute struggle will not remind people of a cat fight. Really, "modernism" has no quarrel with any church that will croon lullabies to a sin-loving world instead of warning men "to flee from the wrath to come."

WHY NOT MEET THE ISSUE FAIRLY?

It is as cheap as it is common—this waving aside the arguments of creationists with the plea that we are ignorant and the foes of science. Let me write this large.

Alibi, Lullaby, By-By

WE COULD ACCEPT EVERY GUESS THEY HAVE EVER MADE AS TO THE AGE AND NAME OF EVERY BONE THEY HAVE EVER FOUND AND UNLESS THEY CALL SOME BONE "ADAM," THEY CANNOT CLAIM TO KNOW WHAT HE WAS LIKE. Even if they fill the prehistoric wilderness with Eoanthropus, Sivapithecus and any other 'pus and 'cus, all these could not prevent, but *would more likely challenge God to make one pair that could fellowship with God.* If God is only big enough to create an amoeba, then the evidence is against us, but a God bigger than the mind of an evolutionist, could have made a man, and if he did, some other bones would not disprove it. Let them find in every hillside a dirty cave littered with bones; such discoveries could no more prove the impossibility of the Eden pair, than the finding of empty sauerkraut cans could prove there never was a can of pineapple.

Let the reader keep in mind that evolutionists say the "Trinil man," the "Piltdown man," the "Neanderthal man" and perhaps the "Heidelberg man" *left no descendants.* In that case, their bones could prove nothing more than a presumption that our ancestors had "low brow" neighbors—if it proved that. While I do not accept the guesses of evolutionists as to these "men," I do admit that there were other characters mingled with the Adamic race to the sorrow of God and the corruption of man. The Bible vouches for the God-likeness of but two early characters and *not even them, after Teacher Nachash showed them how to evolve into gods and know more.* Read the 3rd and 6th chapters of Genesis, keeping in mind that Nachash and Nephilim (translated "serpent" and "giants") were very likely man-like neighbors of Adam's family. In saying this, I do not doubt that Satan used the first and I admit the reference to Nephilim is obscure. If scientists find bones and theorize them into man-like races that lived in the far past, *what of it?* The God of the rainbow and Milky Way could have another—an image-man not cradled in the arms of a brute in the stench of a dirty cave.

In their eagerness to discredit the Bible, evolutionists put a heavy strain on credulity. In the Scientific American for April, 1927, an article supports the theory that some-

Many people do not know that "Eden" in the Old Testament and "Paradise" in the New are translations of the same word. When the Hebrew word for Eden was translated into Greek, they used a word that has come into English as "Paradise." Let the Bible Student be warned that when you give up Eden in the Old Testament, you have logically surrendered Paradise in the New. The "Tree of Life" in Eden is the same as the "Tree of Life" in Paradise.

Many people do not know that Eden, mentioned six times in Genesis is mentioned seven times in other books of the Old Testament. If you decide that it was a myth in Genesis, it is no less a myth in other places. When you start unravelling the Bible (in your own unbelief) there is nothing certain left *for you* this side of judgement, but maxims for "modernists" — maxims that have no more authority than the good advice of heathen philosophers.

time after our ancestors passed the reptile age, they lived on insects. The writer speaks of hitherto unknown skulls found in the Gobi Desert and with such fossils to guide him, proceeds to tell their fortune, so to speak.

They lived on insects.

They lived 10,000,000 years ago.

They layed eggs that were my ancestors or nearly so.

When the eggs hatched, the young ones lived on milk.

The writer knows what they evolved from and what they evolved into.

God had made some marvelous creatures and I do not deny that some have been of a Leghorn-Jersey type—a potential custard factory, but what bothers me is that all that information could come from two skulls, one of them dead for a hundred thousand centuries. I am increasingly amazed at what people doubt in the Bible and what they believe because it is labeled "science."

OUR INHERITANCE

I have 2 parents, 4 grandparents, 8 great grandparents and so on back until the ratio is reversed because of the marriage of relatives. I came into the world with the warp and bias and bent that was my heritage from thousands of ancestors in the 60 centuries of the life stream that flowed from Adam to me. I am a composite in varying proportions of all that these added to or subtracted from the stream that came to me. When I drew the first breath, what there was of me took up the burden of what there was in me—my legacy of human nature—planted with germs of toil and tears, sickness and sin. The life that throbbed in me though wrapped with a new individuality, was *as old as my first ancestor and began then.* Over my cradle there brooded the past, like a ghost from the great abyss of human failure and *demanded reincarnation in me,* but with the past, there hovered an angel waiting to whisper that within me was the marred image of the first Father—God—who called me back from a runaway world that He might refashion that image and make me His heir.

Glory hallelujah!

Hopeful kinsfolk magnified the nobility of the princely men and queenly women back of me and held them up as ideals—and I thank God for traditions that beckon us to the heights—but better than sifted biographies that magnify the good and minimize the bad, is the faith that though my life came by way of cabin or cave, it began in the Garden of God.

Because I began in the Paradise described in Genesis, I am called to the Paradise revealed in Revelation. From Eden lost to Eden restored, this hope that spans the ruins of the ages is my rainbow of promise set against the background of God's grief and man's tears—the triumphal arch to welcome fallen men back to God.

BIRTHRIGHT OR POTTAGE

They would rob me of my birthright to a part in Adam who was the Son of God (Luke 3:38), and make me the heir of a succession of brutes that sinks lower and lower as it fades into the past, *until it is lost somewhere in steaming swamps beyond my reptile sires.*

God forbid!

Must I believe that millions of generations were necessary to bring life from amoeba to me and seek inspiration in the theory that the part of me that is life, *lived in all those ancestors,* and shudder at the mountain of bugs and flies I have eaten and the terrors I knew when I lived in the persons of my ancestors, among the snakes and lizards and sharks of a pitiless past?

Yet they say science will be strangled if they are not permitted to thrust this nightmare upon little children who might otherwise believe that their ancestry went back to God without reptile detour.

If there was no other hell, God could make one by adopting such a system and running it backwards through all the creeping crawling slippery mess till all were deflated, evaporated and united in one amoeba washed up against a smoking shore. If that were hell, evolutionists would cry for mercy. *If it was taught that only one race was evolved from reptiles, it would start a war.*

When faith and foolishness are twins, then can you destroy that part of the Bible that touches the ground (Gen. 2:7-8) and leave the rest hanging in the air.

18

WHAT NO ONE KNOWS

Who can know that any alleged evidence from fossils, refers to a period AFTER the creation described in the Bible? Who can know what events God may have left out when he passed from the first to the second verse of the Bible? Who can know what creations may have then been submerged when the earth was "waste and void"? God has not told us all His experience with worlds and the silences of God are vast enough to lose all the speculations of man. The vast depths of knowledge that man has not tapped, ought to rebuke the cocksureness of man when he would replace revelation with theories. "Let God be found true, but every man a liar." (Rom. 3:4).

TWO METHODS—THIN AND THINNER

There are two guesses (with variations) as to how man came to the top of the evolutionary stew-pot, ready to be skimmed off for heaven, or any other place that evolutionists have not abolished. Neither guess is reasonable; one denies the other; *both are "scientific"*. To make a man out of an ape in one generation would be a miracle, and no undiluted miracle can be tolerated by an undiluted evolutionist. Therefore, one theory divides its miracle into installments *so small that they only tax the imagination;* the other theory thins out the impossible so that it can percolate through geological ages.

What we may call the installment plan, depended upon a succession of freaks, each attended by seven kinds of persistent luck. It makes man the freak of a freak of a freak of the apes, *or whatever the brute was that was farthest from reptiles and nearest man.*

Note: Apparently there is something about apes and monkeys that makes them not exactly acceptable to fastidious evolutionists as ancestors. Many teachers chafe at the suggestion of this relationship and rebuke us for *mistaking their cousins for their grandsires.* Now it would be very easy to quote from eminent evolutionists that some sort of ape was our ancestor. In the Scientific American, May, 1923, there is a diagram that shows the P r o p l i o p i t h e c u s as the ancestor of man. They describe this forefather as a "man-formed" ape. However, I waive the point. Who cares whether we grew on the ape limb or the one next to it, if *they insist that farther back we came from reptiles.* If the reader knows just what brute did preceed man, let him substitue that "varmint" for ape in this discussion. Because that Proplio-person is so hard to spell, let me use the shorter word and accept my apology.

Every stockman knows that freaks appear in the herd

and that by segregation he can modify color, size, shape and product of his animals. He knows that the freak, left to itself, will no more affect the future of the herd than a white blackbird will modify the color of the flock. He knows that he cannot breed his sheep backward or forward to be anything that is not a sheep. If freaks left to themselves *could* become other kinds of animals, we might expect two-headed calves and three-legged chickens to beget similar freaks. If freak added to freak could transform ape (or whatever it was) to man, the process would need a dallying providence surpassing a miracle.

Luck No. 1. Two similar freaks must be born about the same time.
Luck No. 2. They must be born in nearly the same place.
Luck No. 3. They must be male and female.
Luck No. 4. They must survive when the death rate was high.
Luck No. 5. The male must be enamored of the freak female.
Luck No. 6. He must vanquish all rivals, some older and more experienced.
Luck No. 7. They must be segregated or the little apricots will mate back into the main brotherhood.

This multiplied luck or accident or providence must attend every eruption of freakishness. I find that the magazine quoted above, suggests very guardedly that it might be in this order—apes, man-like apes, ape-like men and men. As for me, I can believe that a God big enough for a universe could work a big enough miracle to create a man, but I cannot believe such a God would breed reptiles and marsupials and Propliopithecuses with a view to filling heaven by the way of freaks.

THINNER

The other "scientific" method is that it all happened so gradually that there was not in any generation a perceptible difference from what preceded or followed. We may indicate it this way. There appeared an ape (or whatnot) that was, let us say 99% ape and 1% man. Now in nature as we know it, this mannishness would disappear in subsequent generations just as a white feather in a sparrow's tail fails to modify the sparrow multitude. However, if you wish evolution to work, *you must give it the benefit of the doubt,*

20

and we will take it for granted that all the progeny maintained that 1%.

After 10,000 years (more or less) the 99-1 combination produced an individual that was 98% ape—2% man. Thus the freakishness percolated or percol-aped through hundreds of thousands of births until enough ape filtered out and enough man oozed in from nowhere, to enable the mixture to pass for human.

TROUBLESOME QUESTIONS

Who knows whether we are yet 100% men?

If we are 100% men, can we go on to 110%?

Why did all the intermediate combinations die out?

Why do not more apes, or whatever they were, come a freaking heavenward?

Among the millions of kinds of creatures, why is there not one that evolutionists can freely predict its next evolutionary transformation?

OPOSSUM-LIKE ANCESTORS

The sponsors for this ancestral circus parade have made much of a few bones of theoretical "missing links" between brute and man, but there was one performer in the pageant that was so independent that *it had nothing to hook a link on*. In the succession of ancestors there is presumed to have been a marsupial. Somewhere back in the dissatisfied past, after our forefathers ceased to be reptiles, they were equipped like opossums. The female opossum has a large apron pocket into which she thrusts her new-born babies. In all nature there is no arrangement more useful for the creatures that have it. The theory of evolution *cannot do without it and they cannot do anything with it*. That pocket is so unique, so complete, so independent that there is no way to hook a link that is less than a pocket or more than a pocket, into it. Before the animal had it, there was no possible process by which it could get it. After an animal had it, there would be no conceivable reason for getting rid of it. If our ancestors had this convenient pocket nursery, *how could* they get rid of it, leaving no trace, and

21

hold on to "gill-slits" 50,000,000 years older? It would only be a nuisance unless it was in the right place, open the right way and with a mother knowing exactly how to use it. Let the scientists remove this pouch from the mother opossum and sew it on a mother cat and *both litters will die.* With the appearance of the first baby-pocket, there would have been no succeeding generation of that type, *unless the mother knew exactly how to use it. There never could have been an almost marsupial with an almost instinct getting ready to use an almost pocket to hatch an almost egg or shelter an almost born litter.* I mention the egg because some will say that the pouch was first used as a hatchery. If it was first used for eggs, there would need to be buttons on it unless the animal knew enough not to go down a tree head first. In all nature there is not a reptile getting a marsupium nor an animal getting rid of it. Would any process guided by intelligence, put such a convenience on our ancestors in one age and take it off in the next? Would evolution begin construction of an equipment 50,000 years before it could be used?

Why do evolutionists bluff their way past the obviously impossible? Why not be generous with us and admit two or three miracles?

Because even one miracle would prove the existence of an old fashioned God, able to raise us from the dead and bring us into judgment.

MIRACLE

God is a Spirit. He cannot have eyes, ears and brain as science understands these words. If God can see without such eyes, hear without such ears, think without such a brain, He is the transcendent miracle of the universe. To admit the existence of a non-material intelligent God is to admit that man—apart from revelation—can know as little about God as an oyster knows about flowers and music. Once admit that God is a Spirit and you admit an empire of spirit vastly greater than the universe of stars.

REASON OR TREASON

The more limitations a man thinks he puts on God, the more license he thinks is due to himself. If pushing his

22

There are few original thinkers in the world. Many echo-men think they are saying something new when they re-mouth the theories of their school, their editors, their books or their heroes. When you see a spotted calf, you can easily believe it belongs to the spotted cow, *unless it is a half-breed*. Look at the cartoon again; you did not see it all the first time.

23

brain two inches farther from his "gill-slits" evolves a man from a beast, then three inches may stimulate a man to do the thinking for a God who has no brain. It was inevitable that the anti-Bible revolt that denied man was made in God's image and fell, would be followed by the many detached finger-snappers, eating the bread of the church and denying its faith. We have recently had the spectacle of a popular writer occupying the pulpit of a Kansas City church and daring God to strike him dead. Not many months ago a bishop classified Jesus along with Santa Claus. A dignitary of a great church has explained away a prophecy not to his taste by saying it was written by a Jew (Paul) who had been eating mince pie. Indeed, this book might be filled with stories of men paid to be leaders in institutions founded by Christians—men who wear the name of Christ and openly flout the teachings of the Bible.

WHAT SHALL THE HARVEST BE?

The writer has witnessed an ordination service where the candidates were required to give affirmative answer to the question, "Do you unfeignedly believe all the canonical Scriptures of the Old and New Testaments?" As a part of the ceremony, they knelt at the altar and placed their hands upon the open Bible. An aged minister who participated in the service, suggested that any who decided in after years not to keep faith with the church, *"ought to quit lying or quit preaching."*

If the Bible is a collection of folk-lore, traditions, interpolations, exaggerations, wornout doctrines and an uncertain amount of inspired matter, then it follows that the less of it you believe, the less likely you are to be the victim of a hoax. When a man decides that the God portrayed in the first part of the Bible is a fictional character, there is no logical stopping place till he fixes up a God to his own notion.

A chick will not be bigger than the incubator; a casting will not be greater than the foundry and *a brain-made god will not bulge the walls of its bone cradle.*

If there is no everlastingly dependable revelation of the intelligence that makes playthings of burning worlds, then we must have as many figment-gods as there are god-fixing minds. If we have a national god, it must be a kind of symposium-god.

As for me, I want no Deity that is in any way subject to my criticism. I will have no chameleon god that takes on a color scheme from the background of the Sunday newspaper. Let me shelter under the wings of Jehovah who never wrecked a nation that accepted Him and never for long prospered the nation that insulted Him.

THE KINGDOM OF SKULL

Recently, I heard the head of a great university speaking to about a thousand clergymen. The central thought of his message was, "I am not my body; my body is mine." If he had only said, "I am not the top of my body; the top of my body is mine," I should have understood that he regarded the brain as an accessory, not a dictator to censor revelation. Brain is only 4 degrees away from delirium, one bump from unconsciousness, one pint from intoxication and one hypodermic removed from coma. It is a gift from God, meant to be worthy such a giver, but never meant to be self-sufficient or a rival of revelation. When it is weaned from a dependence on God, it is not so safe a guide for man as an ant's brain is for ants. Without a fixed anchorage outside itself, man is no safer than a storm driven vessel on a lee shore with a crew that carries the anchor downstairs and hooks it in the coal pile. That soul is swindled that gives up the old faith to be guided by a skull—living or dead.

It is now considered quite proper to compliment Jesus, even if one discredits the Book of which he is the living embodiment. They think of Him and the Book as a peerless flower in a broken crock.

Some even acknowledge His Deity though they deny the reliability of the only record of His life. He said, "If ye believed Moses, ye would believe me: for he wrote of me. But if ye believe not his writings, how shall ye believe my words?" This page could be covered with such quotations, but what is the use? The Bible sifter who can reject this, can reject them all.* If no one knows how much of the Bible is true, how can anyone know that any of it is true that is not attested by outside evidence? If you can deny the

---
*See John 5:39,46; Luke 16:31; Matt. 5: 18.

authenticity of the Holy Scriptures and have left a consistent faith in Christ, you can take away the candle and leave the flame, destroy the harp and play on the strings, rub out the colors and keep the picture.

PROVING THE PUDDING

They say, "The proof of the pudding is in the eating." Even so, but it takes a nation at least two generations to digest a pudding, and the nation has a high fever already. Toadstool puddings declare themselves in the obituaries and it would be well for the zealous looseners of religious authority to read the obituaries of nations to some purpose. I have no doubt that "modernists" hope to save the world with high ideals, patriotism, education, public sentiment and such by-products of religion, but to take away divine authority and expect high ideals is like expecting the boys

to build a high fence to keep themselves out of a melon patch. If we have only an indefinite uncertain some-how-or-other God who will not call us to a stern reckoning, we are not likely to invent ideals to hinder our natural bent. Nations have piled up great fortifications, floated great navies, levied great armies, only to collapse because, like a great tree, they have displayed good bark and had a rotted heart.

In Deut. 31:16, God uses an unpleasant expression to upbraid the nation that wearied of its old fashioned God. God is not overly polite to traitors. *There is a prophecy goes with it that is not yet too old to do business.*

26

THE SECOND GENERATION

If a man develops his faith *before* he borrows his doubts as to the reliability of the Bible, he may retain a faith in the God of the Bible, but, WATCH THE SECOND GENERATION OF DOUBT COLLECTORS.

That is not original with me. Great men have said it in other words.

About once a week some man gets his name in the papers by announcing great improvement in the morals of the nation. That is "news" to a newspaper and needs many repetitions to be convincing. The Cleveland Plain Dealer, Dec. 22, 1927, says the inmates of penal institutions in Ohio have increased from 2561 in 1919 to 9144 in 1927. Our keen minded young people are following the current teachings of theatres, magazines and schools to a logical conclusion.

THE ENTHRONEMENT OF THE APE

An Alliance newspaper dated Dec. 5, 1927, reports an event at a near-by college that is under church auspices. It says that the students piled several thousand books in a room and "In the center of the chaos, Bibles had been stacked, with a stuffed ape taken from the college museum seated on top holding in his outstretched paws a copy of Darwin's origin of species."

Now where would they get such an idea?

In the same city it is reported that a high school student said in a public debate on evolution, "When the Bible was written, God did not know anything about science."

Arguments Against

How would the son of a clergyman get such a notion?

The Cleveland Plain Dealer of April 7, 1927, prints on the sport page, between prize-fight stories, the announcement that the alumni of a college (under church auspices) will have "their annual spring dinner dance," and that "A team of thirteen star swimmers, all girls from the college, will stage an exhibition of swimming and diving." In a previous issue, the paper said that leading members of the faculty were coming to the city for the event.

Have they no boy swimmers?

Certainly, but boys do not stage an exhibition so interesting to gentlemen visitors.

Well, what of it? Was there anything in the alleged ages of evolution that made sex exhibitions undesirable? Are our nearest of kin among the brutes handicapped with clothing?

And yet, this school was built with the money of Christians who thought they descended from Adam.

A missionary writes me from South Africa that many young people have adopted the slogan, "Let yourself go!" Very acceptable advice to young or old who find religious restraint irksome.

The nation is fairly top-heavy with information that exalts human skill and tends to make God less and less necessary to people who know how to do for themselves, but we are slow to learn that a nation guided only by public senti-

28

ment is like a ship that follows the reflection of its own lights upon the water. For 6,000 years men have tinkered with laws and nations have wabbled to and fro between democracy and despotism and they are not yet satisfied. I have lived long enough to see people glory in conditions that shocked them in the previous decade.

The world needs a permanent God that it believes in. No nation can long do business if every man uses a yardstick, a bushel measure and a pound weight *that is about what he thinks is fair.* Society cannot long stay honest with dollars that are worth 90c to one man, 80c to another, 70c to another, and so on down the scale to nothingness. If one "Christian" accepts 90% of the Bible, another 80%, another 70%, *where will it end?* Already we have samples of *leaders on display who accept* 100% *of themselves and any fraction of the Bible that agrees with them.* If the nation follows such leadership, it will end not far from where the buzzards begin. A nation that turns its back on God, turns its face toward the junk-pile.

BIBLE OR BABEL

Blessed Book of God! Though it was written in man's imperfect language and translations can only approximate the exact meaning, yet it has been the torchlight of civilization. Have you noticed that the ambitious men who would dim the torch, *are in the lightning-bug business?* The man who specializes on the fallibility of the Bible never purposely advertises his own fallibility.

I could wish no greater national blessing than a revival in the halls of Congress with every member weeping because of the nation's sins. If I could have another wish, it would be that our anti-Bible "Christians" might have an island of their own and take the birth control advocates with them.

Arguments Against

Some accept 90% of the Holy Scriptures, some 80%, some less, some nothing; will the children slide farther than father thinks is safe? We may not expect perfection of translators and copyists, but when you start sliding where will you stop slipping?

Five books indicated here are the same size and price as the one you are reading. We send them postpaid for 20c each. Stamps accepted, coin preferred. "The Reunion" is 8 pages and is one of the tracts we give free with a dollar order. Dollar bill or check will do.

After you have ordered any book at 20c you can buy 10 or more of that book for distribution at half price, but not less than ten of one kind at half price.

Name 3 books and we will send you 2 of each (3 to read, 3 to loan), for one dollar.

All books postpaid except orders of 50 or more at special prices.

HOMO PUB. CO.

Rogers, O.

31

THEY EXHORT US TO "WAKE UP"

Only about one in five cares.

Thousands of our finest young people go from Christian homes to so-called Christian Colleges, builded and maintained with Christian money and come back with their faith warped, perverted or shattered. One phase of this betrayal is camouflaged by the clever representation that it is the "REVOLT OF YOUTH," when it is only TEACHER PROPAGANDA come to the surface. They hope you are dull enough to believe that this "movement" just naturally HATCHED ITSELF OUT OF ITS OWN EGG. Even these choice young people do not suspect that it is what in street parlance is call a "plant" and that old he-Miriams are hid in the bullrushes. A cute little slogan has been fixed up for them—"WAKE UP GRANDPA."

We hope grandpa wakes up.

The writer has a long letter from such a student from a Christian home. He asks, "Why are young people so apt to accept science and abandon faith?" Of course, it is for the same reason that a sailor's parrot is apt to swear, but this fine lad thinks it happens because it HAS TO HAPPEN. He proceeds to show to his own satisfaction the superiority of science and evolution over the Bible. He makes it clear (to himself) that God Almighty must keep up with the latest trend of thought or be left behind.

The entire letter reveals a woeful ignorance of what the Bible really says and an amazing familiarity with what its critics have said. There was only one argument that the writer had not heard 30 years ago in the infidel home of his boyhood.

We are selling books at the cost of printing, advertising and mailing. We know of no books on such subjects more eagerly read by young people and tired workers who shun the severely classical books that bristle with profound phrases. These books are doing much good or much harm. If it is good, why not order a supply to loan or give away; if they work mischief, please get someone to answer them. If you believe the author is ignorant, it will be a play-spell for some leader to answer one. Try it.

Arguments Against

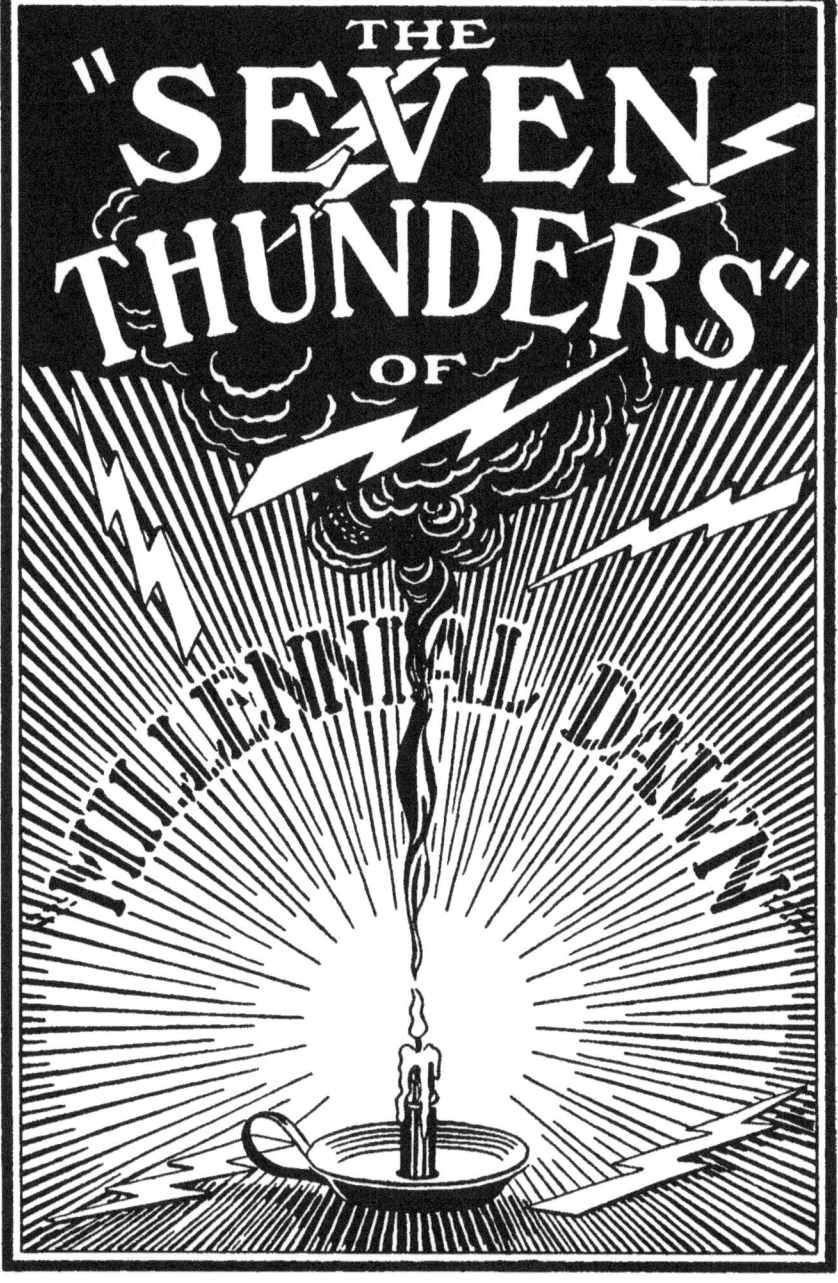

Arguments Against

The "Seven Thunders" of Millennial Dawn

Arguments Against

JUST TO TELL YOU WHY

It is not my purpose to fling words at Russellism.
What I hope to do is to call back some of its own words that it would like to forget, and let it tell its own blunders.

I have no quarrel with the credulous followers of Mr. Russell; they have denied so many of my statements that I have reason to believe they are really not well informed about their own history as a cult.

I have made something of a study of cults and isms and my conviction is that *God compels every outstanding heresy to carry exposed threads that will* RAVEL IT OUT *for prayerfully thoughtful people.*

Man is prone to gullibility, else our Lord would not have said "Take heed that ye be not deceived." I have seen men stand in line waiting to feed money into a gambling device that was set against them. I have known a pretty woman on trial for the murder of her husband, to employ a secretary to answer proposals of marriage. You can find devotees following man-made theories on every level, from abysmal folly to sublime conceit and it does not occur to them that by some possibility, they might be misled.

If the Russell-Rutherford guesses had been the vagaries of some old settler who predicted events by goose bones, black cats, dog howling or the tilt of a new moon, we might dismiss them with a smile, but these men presumed to unscare sin-lovers who feared to meet an offended God, and their *promises* persisted when their *prophecies* failed.

In a dim light, you can frighten people by putting a time fuse in a green pumpkin, but the hoax becomes apparent when the explosion of the improvised bomb is long overdue. My contention is that someone put new fuses into the pumpkins. Now I have no doubt that many people have occasion to fear the wrath of God, but the pity is that fleeing from a false alarm they have taken refuge in the shadow of a slumbering volcano.

Let me assure the reader that I have no objection to the resurrection of the dead and the translation of the saints before the end of 1914—or any other year that pleases God—but the menace of these prophecies was that they were used to frighten or bribe people into accepting soul deceiving heresies.

When the 1914 bomb failed to explode Mr. Russell warped some words of the language to fit the failure. In the foreword of Vol. 2, dated 1916, he explained that the Gentile Times "CHRONOLOGICALLY ENDED" in 1914. Later, Mr. Rutherford employed another verbal subterfuge by saying, " . . . . the old world LEGALLY ENDED in 1914." (emphasis mine). Why not go farther and say that Abraham chronologically raised from the dead and the saints were legally translated in 1914?

Apparently Mr. Rutherford is not wholly satisfied with these efforts to dodge, for he says in his "Harp" book (p 250), "Why should we quibble now about dates?" Since his own predictions for 1925 have failed, I have no doubt he would like very much to UN-QUIBBLE a number of dates.

Of Samuel, the Word says Jehovah "did let none of his words fall to the ground," but Mr. Russell has littered the ground with fallen words and holds the record for the most words and the fewest fulfilments.

Copyright 1928 by B. H. SHADDUCK

INTRODUCTION

By the Editor of *The Sunday School Times*

Dr. Shadduck's books exposing the unscriptural theories of evolution, "Jocko-Homo Heavenbound," "Puddle to Paradise," and "The Toadstool Among the Tombs," are widely known and have had an enormous circulation. Some time ago a number of citizens in his locality who had been furnished free literature on Russellism urged a public debate between Dr. Shadduck and a representative of Millennial Dawn. Arrangements were under way for such a debate, but when the Russellites presented in writing their propositions governing the debate, they were found to include the following:

That B. H. Shadduck furnish a bond of $500 as guarantee that he will not . . . refer to any quotation contained in any periodical or book published by the International Bible Students Association, and if B. H. Shadduck shall . . . refer to any quotation or book published by the International Bible Students Association he shall at once pay the sum of $500 to his opponent in this debate.

That ended the negotiations. The followers of "Pastor Russell" knew that Dr. Shadduck had in his possession several editions of Russell"s books, and would make public exposure of the changes that had been made in these books after Russell's death.

Now the facts that Dr. Shadduck would have brought out in that debate, before a few hundred listeners, are given to the world-wide family of readers of The Sunday School Times, in the earnest hope that they may save multitudes of God's people from the snare and injury that this unscriptural cult has proved itself to be.

Note by the author: The major portion of this book is a reprint of articles that appeared serially in *The Sunday School Times*. In that presentation, the author tried to conform to standards of literary excellence maintained by that defender of the faith. The cartoons and other matter that have been added to fill out the book, are more in the characteristic style of the author and for these, the Editor shares no responsibility.

The Seven Thunders of Millennial Dawn

BY B. H. SHADDUCK, Ph. D.

The "Seven Thunders" are seven books. The name is not my invention; the seventh volume reveals it.

These are not just rhetorical thunders or some literary cannonading; they are the Seven Thunders of the Book of Revelation—if Volume 7 is to be believed.

These books were published by Charles T. Russell (known as "Pastor Russell"), one at a time, the first in 1886, the last in 1917. Volume 7 was published after Mr. Russell's death, and is called "Posthumous Work of Pastor Russell." When the earlier volumes were issued the series was called "Millennial Dawn"; later the series was called "Studies in the Scriptures."

Not only are these books identified by their writer as the Seven Thunders of Revelation, but they are said to be the Seven Angels, the Seven Plagues, the Great Chain in the hands of the angel, the Seven Vials of the wrath of God, and the Amethyst, which was "Pastor Russell's birthstone" and the jewel in the twelfth foundation of the New Jerusalem. Volume 7 claims for itself that it is the Golden Censor, the Great Winepress of the wrath of God, "that will squeeze the juice out of the 'abominations of the earth'," and the point of the Sword of the Spirit. Readers wishing to examine these claims are referred to Volume 7 (also called "The Finished Mystery"), pages 167, 237, 320, 299, 237, 326, 327, 145, 229, and 466.

THUNDERS OR BLUNDERS?

It is not my purpose to make sport of these books. It will be enough to let them speak for themselves. It is my conviction that thousands of sincere people have been drawn to the organization founded by Mr. Russell because the doctrines deal gently with sin. I write because the world ought to know just how dependable were his claims.

If these books are all that Volume 7 says they are, they take rank with the Word of God; if they are a human patchwork of prophecies that have failed, then they partly fulfill the prophecy of our Lord Jesus, "And many false prophets shall rise, and shall deceive many."

4

That the leaders of the Millennial Dawn people know of the extravagant claims and unfulfilled prophecies of these books is evident from their efforts to keep the facts from the public. When the writer would have met them in public debate in 1926, and they learned that he possessed an early edition of these books and a later edition with changed dates, they refused to proceed unless he would give bond in

> 9. That Mr. B.H. Shadduck D.D. furnish a bond of $500.00 as a guarantee that he will not slander Pastor Russell during this debate, or refer to any quotation contained in any periodical or book published by the International Bible Students Association, and if the Rev. B.H. Shadduck shall slander Pastor Russell or refer to any quotation or book published by the International Bible Students Association he shall at once pay the sum of $500.00 to his opponent in this debate
> 10. That it be understood that to slander means: To circulate a malicious report

the sum of five hundred dollars not to "refer to any quotations contained in any periodical or book published by the International Bible Students Association." After reading some of the quotations that follow, one can understand why they did this.

HISTORY OF THE MOVEMENT

In 1844 a cult under the leadership of William Miller announced the coming of the Lord in that year. Let it be said to the credit of this earnest man that when his prophecies utterly failed he did not try to insert other dates and perpetuate the mistake, as did Mr. Russell and his followers. That Mr. Russell was the successor of Mr. Miller, and did continue the Miller movement in revised form, his followers vehemently deny, but I offer the testimony of these books to prove that Mr. Russell believed that he had discovered Mr. Miller's mistakes in that our Lord would come thirty years later and be invisible. Volume 3, page 86, says: "We recognize that movement [Miller's] as being in God's order . . . This was undoubtedly of the Lord's providence . . . it was the beginning of the *right* understanding of Daniel's visions and at the right time to fulfill prophecy."

In Volume 7, page 163, Mr. Miller is said to be the voice that gave orders to the sixth angel described in the ninth chapter of Revelation, and on page 167 Mr. Russell is said to be the voice that followed, as described in the next chapter of Revelation. In reading Mr. Russell's books, I find that, for them, language can never be depended on to mean what ordinary people understand it to mean, but if language can be taken at its face value it is clear, from the quotations above, that Mr. Russell regarded Mr. Miller as a kind of forerunner of himself. I have pointed out the obvious connection between these two movements in order to emphasize the fact that the "scares" of one were no more dependable than those of the other.

ARE THE FOLLOWERS OF RUSSELL A SECT?

It seems to hurt the feelings of the followers of Russell to call them a sect or speak of them as his followers, and as I would not be charged with discourtesy I refer them to pages 84, 126, and 142 in Volume 7, where occur the expressions, "Pastor Russell's followers," "followers of Pastor Russell," and " a follower of the Reformer, Charles T. Russell." They have named themselves "International Bible Students Association," and insist that they differ from sects because they "go by the Bible." They think this ought to settle it. Now it would be a remarkable coincidence if all of

6

these people in many lands, by independent Bible study, arrived at an understanding that many dreadful events would occur *before* 1914, and then the same people by independent study discovered that they had miscalculated and that the correct date was 1915, and later on discovered it was 1918, and still later found it was 1925, *and not one of the dates prove correct.* It would be amazing if "going by the Bible" would convince all these people that certain measurements in the Great Pyramid proved that the world's great trouble would begin in 1874, and then by the same independent Bible study find that the same pyramid shows that the trouble was to start in 1914. Would not such remarkable agreement in making mistakes suggest that they are a Russell Students Association?

SELF-COMMENDATION

No book of the Bible makes such sweeping claims for itself as this "Finished Mystery," Volume 7, which claims to be the embodiment of at least seven prophecies in the Book of Revelation and undertakes to explain all that was hitherto hidden in Ezekiel, Canticles, and Revelation. It says (p. 466), "The Sword of the Spirit was to be wielded by Pastor Russell twice three times in his six volumes." It explains that itself *is the point of the sword.* The inference is that before Volume 7 was issued there was no point to the sword. Other Bible students know that the "sword of the Spirit" is the Word of God.

One may expect that a book that recommends itself so highly will exalt the alleged author to some station far above any other prophet. Though it was printed after Mr. Russell had "passed from earth" and mentions Mr. Russell by name no less than 232 times (I have not numbered the pronouns), the publisher says (p. 5), *"He did write it."* The same page says, "Pastor Russell was a man of unusual modesty," all of which leaves the authorship in some doubt.

On page 144 this book, which is called a "Posthumous Work of Pastor Russell," explains Revelation 8:3, which describes an angel offering incense, by saying, *"This verse shows that, though Pastor Russell has passed beyond the veil, he is still managing every feature of the Harvest work"* (italics mine). Page 169 says, "Pastor Russell was

7

Arguments Against

the seventh angel" mentioned in the tenth chapter of Revelation. On page 334 we are told that the angel mentioned in Revelation 22:6 is "the same angel mentioned in Revelation 1:1;19:9,10; representing Pastor Russell beyond the veil." Page 53 says of him, "He has privately [why privately?] admitted his belief that he was chosen for his great work from before his birth." Page 418 identifies Mr. Russell as the "man in linen" seen by Ezekiel. If the reader will open a Bible at Ezekiel 9 and read of this character who marked the foreheads of those who were to be spared, and was followed by six men with "slaughter weapons," he can better understand the claim that this "man in linen" was none other than Mr. Russell himself, shown to Ezekiel in a vision something near 2,500 years ago. It appears that Mr. Russell has already finished this marking, for page 420 says he has "undoubtedly made his report in the presence of Christ that he has done the work he was given to do."

I would not think this a fit place to refer to the troubles Mr. Russell had with his wife, but the book proclaims it. Volume 7 gives to them eternal significance. In Ezekiel 24 is a story of the death of the prophet's wife,—at least most people would so understand it,—which this book says has reference to the trouble between Mr. and Mrs. Russell. Page 483 offers as an exposition of Ezekiel 24:15,16: "God took away from Pastor Russell the desire of his eyes, her whom he loved, with a stroke or 'plague' of spiritual error that completely separated them." Thus it appears that the divorce case of Mr. Russell was typed or foretold in the Book of Ezekiel.

Not only is Mr. Russell identified as the angel or angels who appeared to the apostle John, but he is said to be the "loud voice" of Revelation 10:3, the "great voice" of Revelation 16:1, and the "strong voice" of Revelation 18:2 (pp. 167, 237, 273). If the reader will read these portions of Revelation and see that these voices are ascribed to the Lord Jesus in the first, from within the Temple in the second, and an angel of great power in the third reference, he may decide how near this comes to blasphemy.

The edition of the book that I have carries the imprint "393,000 edition," which indicates that a great army of people accept these interpretations as the voice of the seventh angel, and think of themselves as "Bible students." After reading the repeated warnings of our Lord in Matthew 24:4, 11, 24, that "false prophets shall rise, and shall deceive many," I am better prepared to believe it possible to find buyers for a "393,000 edition" of this "Finished Mystery."

Here are samples from this volume that indicate the estimate these people have of other people who may think themselves Bible students. "In 1878 the stewardship of the things of God, the teaching of Bible truths, was taken from the clergy, unfaithful to their age-long stewardship, and given to Pastor Russell" (p. 386). "Then, in 1881, he became God's watchman for all Christendom" (p. 387). This will explain why these people never had any other "pastor." On page 227 appears this prayer against other people: "O Lord, judge them with thy Truth! Thou hast called them the 'abominations of the earth,' and so they are. Bring their man-made clergy-ridden systems to an end and make their memory to perish from the earth! Amen." Page 410 has this: "The clergy's God is plainly not Jehovah, but the ancient deity, hoary with the iniquity of ages—Baal—the Devil himself."

NIMROD AND THE TRINITY

Their strong dislike for the doctrine of the Trinity is indicated by these samples, from pages 414 and 415 of Volume 7: "Nimrod married his mother, Semiramis, so that, in a sense, he was his own father and his own son. Here was the origin of the Trinity doctrine." "The practices of Nimrod were continued in secret by Semiramis; and as every caution had to be taken, the things done were veiled in mystery. Each act and person were represented only in symbols known to the initiated. Here originated the various secret societies, with their blood curdling oaths of secrecy ... all of them abominations to God." As Nimrod is spoken of in but three verses in the Bible (Gen. 10:8,9; I. Chron. 1:10), none of them even hinting at such behavior. it is evident that these accusations are not the result of Bible study.

"TRUTH PEOPLE" AND "PRESENT TRUTH"

Not only do Millennial Dawn people give themselves the

exclusive name of "Truth People," but they claim the exclusive custody of "Present Truth." This giving of tense modifications to truth is consistent for people who specialize in "truth" that needs to be "set" frequently like a slow going clock. The "truths" that failed them in 1914, 1918, and 1925 have been replaced with a "truth" that has some years yet to go.

DO ANGELS BLUNDER?

Could a man who was chosen before he was born to put ink on the persons who are to be spared, a man who is a central figure in the great visions of Ezekiel and Revelation, a man who is the loud voice of Jesus, the Seventh Angel, the instrument to turn loose the Seven Thunders and pour out the Seven Last Plagues,—could he mislead multitudes?

This is a good place to stop and think.

Mr. Russell prophesied that our churches, schools, banks, and governments would be completely destroyed by October, 1914. Later, the destruction was promised in installments ending in 1925. Volume 4, page 622, says of the kingdom of God: "Its influence and work will result in the complete destruction of 'the powers that be' of 'this present evil world,' political, financial, ecclesiastical—by the close of the 'times of the Gentiles,' October, A. D. 1914." On page 99, Volume 2, he says: "The final end of the kindgoms of this world, and the full establishment of the kingdom of God, will be accomplished by the end of A. D. 1914." Please observe that in these prophecies the words *complete, final end*, and *full establishment* do not admit of any range of option for the events. In an edition of these books showing publisher's date of 1923 the words "by the close" in the first quotation are changed to "about the close," and the words "by the end" in the second quotation are changed to "near the end." Even with these changes the fulfillment is long overdue.

Volume 7 postpones the collapse for four years. It says (p. 485) : "In the year 1918, when God destroys the churches wholesale and the church members by millions, it shall be that any that escape shall come to the works of Pastor Russell [not Judge Rutherford] to learn the meaning of the downfall of 'Christianity'."

10

From this, it appears that survivors will be Russell students—*the very thing these people say they are not.*

Let the reader keep in mind that this Volume 7 was printed the next year after Mr. Russell died, as a "Posthumous Work of Pastor Russell." Therefore it is *the last word* from Mr. Russell on dates and events. I emphasize this because there are books in circulation that have evidently been tampered with—books that *appear to be* wholly the literary work of Mr. Russell written more than twenty years previously—books in which the time limit is, in some cases, lifted or the prophecies modified.

Volume 7 establishes the fact that as late as 1917 all sorts of upheaval, collapse, and calamity were expected in 1918, 1920, 1921, and 1925. This fact ought to nullify the thinly disguised efforts to make the books that were written earlier show a later program of Mr. Russell.

I will not weary the reader with the many prophecies that had movable dates, but I would caution persons having copies of the books that an early publisher's date does not prove that the clumsy revisions that were evidently thrust into a type page already set up were prepared by Mr. Russell before that time. In many cases *the revision is so calculated and measured that it fits into a line without disturbing the first and last words of the line, and rarely does it disturb the lines above and below,* though there are a very few places where a new paragraph is set in. Volume 2, with a publisher's date of 1923, shows a chart on page 247 that dates the destruction of nominal Christendom for 1915. Volume 7, *with a publisher's date five years earlier,* has the same chart on page 595, with the date three years later. Thus it is clear that the earlier publisher's dates may be consorting with the later viewpoint.

THUNDERS RE-THUNDERED

Not only have they reset the doomsday of Christendom, but they have postponed their own departure. Volume 3, early edition, says on page 228, "Just how long before 1914 the last living members of the body of Christ will be glorified, we are not directly informed." Mr. Russell becomes more certain as he writes, and he says on page 364, "We may well accept the testimony of the Great Pyramid, that

11

That the deliverance of the saints must take place some time before 1914 is manifest, since the deliverance of fleshly Israel, as we shall see, is appointed to take place at that time, and the angry nations will then be authoritatively commanded to be still, and will be made to recognize the power of Jehovah's Anointed. Just how long before 1914 the last living members of the body of Christ will be glorified, we are not directly informed; but it certainly will not be until their work in the flesh is done; nor can we reasonably presume that they will long remain after that work is accomplished. With these two thoughts in mind, we can approximate the time of the deliverance.

This is an enlarged photographic reproduction from page 228 in Vol. 3. Please notice that the glorification of the saints MUST happen BEFORE 1914 because the Jews are to be delivered then. Notice that any war after that, will be contrary to Divine commands *"authoritively"* given.

That the deliverance of the saints must take place (very) soon after 1914 is manifest, since the deliverance of fleshly Israel, as we shall see, is appointed to take place at that time, and the angry nations will then be authoritatively commanded to be still, and will be made to recognize the power of Jehovah's Anointed. Just how long (after) 1914 the last living members of the body of Christ will be glorified, we are not directly informed; but it certainly will not be until their work in the flesh is done; nor can we reasonably presume that they will long remain after that work is accomplished. With these two thoughts in mind, we can approximate the time of the deliverance.

This is a similar reproduction from the 1923 edition of the same page and book. Consider that any false prophet since the world began, could have saved his face if permitted to make such significant changes as BEFORE and AFTER, Both reproductions are enlarged.

Arguments Against

the last members of the 'body' or 'bride' of Christ will have been tested and accepted and will have passed beyond the veil before the close of A. D. 1910." The edition dated 1923 makes the first quotation read, "Very soon after 1914"; and the second quotation makes the pyramid testify that "anarchous trouble" is coming on that date.

Mr. Russell's followers chide me for calling attention to these discredited prophecies and remind me that "everybody makes mistakes."

These prophecies are more than mistakes.

They are no less than false prophecies, and false prophecies can only come from false prophets. Their mischief has been multiplied by as many as there have been devotees to peddle them from person to person and from door to door. Since the prophecies failed to come true on the dates set for them, the followers have revised the dates and the things said about the dates, and now they boast that Mr. Russell prophesied the World War.

EXCUSES

Some of Mr. Russell's followers insist that the fact that his prophecies were misdated by a few years does not really affect the truth. But Mr. Russell did not allow for any elasticity in the fulfillment of his forecasts.

He named the exact month of the exact year.

As the very foundation of his system, he declared that the Lord Jesus came to earth in October, 1847, to direct the "Harvest," which was a period of exactly forty years, ending October, 1914. With fanatical zeal his devotees sowed the English-speaking world and many foreign lands with the prophecy that 1914 would be "the farthest limit of the rule of imperfect men." They promised the *full* establishment of the kingdom of God on earth in 1914. If Mr. Russell was mistaken as to what happened at the close of the forty year period, *he must have been mistaken as to what happened at the beginning of the forty years.* Mr. Russell made his prophecies hang on exact fulfillment. In Volume 2, page 243, he says: *"For be it distinctly noticed that if the chronology, or any of these time-periods, be changed but one year, the beauty and force of this parallelism are destroyed"* **(emphasis mine).**

In the face of such a challenge, *some one did change them.* Some one revised the blunders and called them thunders.

Let us hear from God.

Deuteronomy 18:22 says: "When a prophet speaketh in the name of the Lord, *if the thing follow not, nor come to pass, that is the thing which the Lord hath not spoken, but the prophet hath spoken it presumptuously: thou shalt not be afraid of him.*"

If we ignore this challenge of God and excuse Mr. Russell's mistakes on the plea that he was human and his proneness to blunder outweighed his ability to thunder, yet why did the mistakes continue after he had "passed beyond the veil" to "manage every feature of the Harvest work"?

Volume 7, issued after Mr. Russell's death, sets the date for the world's upsetting and the end of the Harvest in 1918. In this revised prophecy, it appears that republics will persist for two years, for page 258 says, "Even the republics will disappear in the fall of 1920."

Young people will not remember the dire upheavals promised before 1914 and later adjusted to 1915, 1918, 1920, 1921, and 1925; and, as later editions are already being offered to discredit my statements, it would be well for older people, who do remember, to commit their testimony to the younger generation. I have not all the editions, but I have enough to show that some statements have been changed twice.

Since they claim that the Lord Jesus came to earth in 1874 to manage the Harvest, and that Mr. Russell went beyond the veil to manage the same Harvest, and the management utterly discredits the prophecies, ought not his followers to entertain some doubt as to the correctness of their doctrines?

FARCICAL EXPOSITIONS

Not only have their "time-periods" utterly failed of fulfillment, so that the calendar testifies against them, but the expositions of Scripture are so trifling that one wonders how normal minds could be enamored of such doctrines. I offer some sample expositions found in Volume 7:

The evil servant of Matthew 24:48 is said to have been a Mr. Barber of Rochester, N. Y. (pp. 54, 386).

15

Arguments Against

The key to the bottomless pit is said to mean the key to *"nothing"* and *"nowhere,"* and John Wesley was given this key (p. 156).

The tails of the locusts mentioned in Revelation 9:3-10 are said to mean Methodist class leaders (p. 159).

The lice that troubled Pharaoh and Egypt are understood to represent The Bible Students Monthly, because this publication causes the people of the world, the Devil, and the clergy to "scratch their heads many a time, wondering how to deal with a plague which they cannot duplicate" (p. 238).

Revelation 18:14 is explained this way: The future of the clergy is that in the Millennial Age they will have to work for a living, like everybody else! Isn't it awful to contemplate? "It means an expense of sixty-five cents for an alarm clock in every preacher's house in Christendom" (p. 285).

In addition to this expense of sixty-five cents, there is a more serious penalty reserved for some of us. Page 338 says, "His penalty will be, when he comes forth from the tomb in the Times of Restitution, that he will have to read the Seven Volumes of Scripture Studies, and get the matter straightened out in his own mind."

Notice that it will be Russell's books, not the Bible, that we must study. Notice also that Judge Rutherford's writings will not be necessary.

The reader may wonder what portion of the Bible means that we shall be punished by being compelled to read these books. The portion referred to is one of the most solemn warnings in the Word of God, Revelation 22:18: "If any man shall add unto these things, God shall add unto him the plagues that are written in this book."

Another verse in Revelation that ought to put a solemn hush on every soul is explained in just such a trifling way. Revelation 14:19 and 20 tells of the "winepress of the wrath of God" and a river of blood reaching sixteen hundred furlongs. Page 230 explains that this Volume 7 (which is the winepress) was printed at Scranton, Pa., and the sixteen hundred furlongs (which are reduced to twelve hundred furlongs for no apparent reason) are said to mean the distance from the printing plant to the headquarters in Brooklyn, N. Y. To make this distance come out right, one must travel by ferry boat and the Lackawanna Railroad. For some years the railroad had a crook in it that made the distance too great, but six years before the book was printed, the railroad company expended twelve million dollars to make a cut-off that made the distance exactly fit the Book of Revelation.

METHODS OF INTERPRETATION

On page 128 of this same Volume 7, there is this corrected (?) prophecy: "There is evidence that the establishment of the kingdom in Palestine will probably be in 1925, ten years later than we once calculated." The reader may be curious to know on what they base their calculation. He may turn to Genesis 15:9 and read the story of a heifer, a she-goat, a ram, turtledove, and a young pigeon. The reasoning is in this fashion:

They decide that the year was 2035 B. C.; on what authority, is not given.

They determine that the total age of these beasts and birds was eleven years, though the age of the birds is guesswork.

For purposes of interpretation, the years are reckoned to have each 360 days—a total of 3,960 days.

They understand each of these days to mean a year.

Add 3,960 years to 2035 B. C., and you have A. D. 1925 —the date of the kingdom of Palestine.

Simple enough! *All that spoiled the method was that it did not happen.*

One weakness of the method is that if the turtledove was two years old, the kingdom is not due till A. D. 2285.

On page 178, they say that "all phases of Babylon will not be disposed of until ten and a half years from the fall of 1914" (the spring of 1925). They base this hope on certain events in the French Revolution.

REASONING IN A CIRCLE

Volume 7, page 5, says, "The Scriptures show that the seventh Volume must be written."

How may we know that the Scriptures mention Volume 7?

Volume 7 says so.

Thus the Bible shows that Volume 7 must be written to show that the Bible says it must be written. How can you argue with a logic like that?

So it is with other astounding interpretations of Scripture. They are sure, because the Scriptures testify that they are the only people who will be able to interpret "present truth."

DEITY OF JESUS REJECTED

After reading in Volume 7 that Mr. Russell for 2,500 years has been a chief actor and speaker in the visions of the prophets, and continues to manage "every feature of the Harvest work," we may expect to find other teachings characteristic of outstanding heresy. On page 161 we are told that the denominations "deny the central truth of the Scriptures," and this central truth is *"that when Jesus Christ came to earth, he came as a man only, devoid of immortality or divinity, that when he died he was as dead as though he had never lived . . ."*

MR. RUSSELL'S CONFESSION

Mr. Russell lived to see the utter failure of the prophecies he had set for "before 1914." In a foreword dated October 1, 1916, printed in an edition of Volume 2, showing publisher's date of 1923, he says: "The author acknowledges that in this book he presents the thought that the Lord's saints might expect to be with him in glory at the ending of the Gentile times . . . October, 1914 . . ." He suggests that "the Lord overruled the mistake for the blessing of His people," and that they *"can praise the Lord—even for the mistake"* (italics mine). In the next paragraph he says, "We drew a false conclusion, however, not warranted by the Word of the Lord." *This is a meager apology for a man who had threatened more people in more ways with more words than any drawer of false conclusions in human history.* This estimate is supported by the claims in this same book that the total of the editions of the seven books is more than twelve million, and the claim in Volume 7 that they are in twenty languages.

18

OTHER FALSE CONCLUSIONS

From Volume 2 (dated 1903) I select the following from pages 76 and 77:

"In this chapter we present the Bible evidence proving that the full end of the times of the Gentiles, *i. e*, the full end of their lease of dominion, will be reached in A. D. 1914; and that date will be the farthest limit of the rule of imperfect men." In the edition dated 1923 this prophecy is cleverly changed to read, "And that date will see the disintegration of the rule of imperfect man." The same volume, early edition, says on pages 77 and 78, "The great 'time of trouble such as never was since there was a nation' will reach its culmination and end at that date . . ." The later edition reads, "will reach its culmination in a world-wide reign of anarchy . . . " The date referred to is 1914. The papacy, which is declared to be "Antichrist" on page 361, is named on page 356 for "final extinction" "near the close of the 'Day of Wrath' . . . 1914." This statement is unchanged in the later edition.

Volume 4, page 625, says: "The beginning of the earthly phase of the kingdom in the end of A. D. 1914 will, we understand, consist wholly of the resurrected holy ones of olden time,—from John the Baptizer back to Abel,—'Abraham, Isaac, Jacob, and all the holy prophets'." On page 619, this resurrection is said to be *"visible."* This is unchanged in the later edition. It is another "false conclusion." It is more than a mistake to promise the visible resurrection of all the holy ones in 1914. It is more than a mistake to rate this man as the loud voice of Jesus (Vol.7, p. 125), and being or sounding the "trump of God" (Vol. 7, p. 385).

REPAIRING THE THUNDERS

Let the reader decide whether it is honest to change the dates in these books and the things said about the dates and leave the public to suppose that they were the original prophecies of Mr. Russell. Let the reader decide whether the seven thunders described in the Book of Revelation could by any possibility need to be changed.

On page 228 of Volume 3 there is a promise that the saints will be delivered and the "last living members" will be glorified "before 1914." In the edition of 1923, the word

19

before is changed to *after*. In the early edition of Volume 4, pages 546 and 547, we find this: "We have seen that God has set a time for every feature of his plan, and that we are even now in the 'Day of Vengeance,' which is a period of forty years; that it began in October, 1874, and will end in October, 1914." Please note that it is a *set* time, *exactly forty years to a month*, and it began in 1874. The edition dated 1923 has changed the last four words to read, "Will end very shortly." *Forty-nine years after this forty-year period began, they announce that it will end very shortly—*the longest forty-year period in history. And now fifty-three years have passed and it is not yet closed.

Volume 2, page 81, early edition, tells of righteousness over the world that "can date only from A. D. 1914." The later edition reads, "Could not precede A. D. 1914." This is certainly fixing it to stay fixed, for *no event in the next million years, which happened after* 1923, *can precede* 1914. In the same manner, a prophecy on page 221, that the Jews "will not be received back into *full favor* until 1914," is changed to read, "After 1915." The Jews can certainly depend on that.

CARELESS WORK

The work must have been done in haste or by someone who overlooked important discrepancies between Mr. Russell and the calendar, for a number of discredited prophecies escaped attention. Here is just one that I find on page 153 of the 1923 edition of Volume 3: "And, with the end of A. D. 1914, what God calls Babylon and men call Christendom will have passed away."

Did Mr. Russell's books tell the date of the World War? They did—after it began.

Three years after the war began I first heard that Mr. Russell had foretold the exact date of the outbreak of the war. When I denied this, they gave me "Studies in the Scriptures," and there it was, *plain enough to astound the unwary.* When I compared these books with the earlier edition called "Millennial Dawn," the hoax was apparent. In "Millennial Dawn," there were very positive statements that all trouble would be over *before* 1914.

CHANGING THE PYRAMID

In the early edition of Volume 3, page 342, certain measurements of the Great Pyramid are given. We are told that these are "the very accurate measurements" made by Professor Smyth in 1872 (p. 338). As a guarantee that Professor Smyth was unquestioned authority, the letters F.R.S.E. and F.R.A.S. follow his name, and Mr. Russell adds his own assurance that this pyramid "witness" fully corroborates the Bible.

From one point to another in one passage of the pyramid, the distance is given as 3,416 inches. Mr. Russell says these inches symbolize years that start with 1542 B. C., and adds: "Thus the pyramid witnesses that the close of 1874 was the *choronological* beginning of the time of trouble such as was not since there was a nation—no, nor ever shall be afterward." In the volume given me after the World War began, the prophecy is made to fit the event, though the books carried a publisher's date prior to 1914. I have explained elsewhere that changes have evidently been made in the books without disturbing the publisher's date.

In the later edition, we have the same assurances that the measurements were very accurate, were made in 1872, and were coroborated by the Bible. There is not a hint that any error has been discovered, *but the number of inches between the given points is changed to* 3,457. Mr. Russell is made to say: "Thus the pyramid witnesses that the close of 1914 will be the beginning of the time of trouble such as was not since there was a nation—no, nor ever shall be afterward."

I do not know who made the changes in these books, but it is significant that in a signed statement of Mr. Russell dated October 1, 1916, and printed as a foreword in the 1923 edition of this same Volume 3, he discusses his former mistaken views exactly as though they had not been corrected. He says of this volume, "Scarcely a word would need to be changed if it were written today—twenty-six years later." He speaks of the same pyramid passage and says it *"still represents figuratively . . . "* (italics mine). That foreword does not approach common honesty, if he excused the mistakes in his prophecies with a plea that they were twenty-six years old, knowing at the time that they had been rad-

21

Arguments Against

a fixed date to mark upon the downward passage. This measure is 1542 inches, and indicates the year B. C. 1542, as the date at that point. Then measuring *down* the "Entrance Passage" from that point, to find the distance to the entrance of the "Pit," representing the great trouble and destruction with which this age is to close, when evil will be overthrown from power, we find it to be 3416 inches, symbolizing 3416 years from the above date, B. C. 1542. This calculation shows A. D. 1874 as marking the beginning of the period of trouble; for 1542 years B. C. plus 1874 years A. D. equals 3416 years. Thus the Pyramid witnesses that the close of 1874 was the *chronological* beginning of the time of trouble such as was not since there was a nation—no, nor

By this enlarged reproduction from page 342 of Vol. 3 (early edition), the reader may see that the Great Pyramid proves that the world's greatest trouble was due to begin in 1874. In the edition of 1923, the same Pyramid proves it was due to begin in 1914. If the war would not fit the Pyramid, the Pyramid must be made to fit the war — easy enough if you know how.

The "Seven Thunders" of Millennial Dawn

downward passage. This measure is 1542 inches, and indicates the year B. C. 1542, as the date at that point. Then measuring *down* the "Entrance Passage" from that point, to find the distance to the entrance of the "Pit," representing the great trouble and destruction with which this age is to close, when evil will be overthrown from power, we find it to be 3457 inches, symbolizing 3457 years from the above date, B. C. 1542. This calculation shows A. D. 1915 as marking the beginning of the period of trouble; for 1542 years B. C. plus 1915 years A. D. equals 3457 years. Thus the Pyramid witnesses that the close of 1914 will be the beginning of the time of trouble such as was not since there was a nation—no, nor ever shall be afterward. And thus it will be noted that this "Witness" fully corroborates the Bible testi-

The Egyptians are very careless with their pyramids and leave them out in the hot sun, but I do not believe that pyramid warped *in Egypt* after the "Dawn" people mis-guessed the war by 40 years. This reproduction from the edition dated 1923 indicates that the pyramid was stretched in the U. S. A. Both editions prove their claim by "very accurate measurements" made in 1872.

ically changed more than thirteen years after they were written. (They are not changed in an edition thirteen years after being written.) In Mr. Russell's foreword dated 1916, printed in Volume 6, I find his statement that he *would* make changes if he were "writing this volume today," but I have never found in any of these books an acknowledgment that changes *had* been made.

A WEAK DEFENSE

I now quote from other forewords dated 1916 and appearing in the editions dated 1923. Twenty-seven years after it was written, Mr. Russell says of Volume 2: "It is not to be considered strange if some suggestions made in this volume have not been fulfilled with absolute accuracy to the very letter." *Considering that it was wholly unfulfilled from cover to cover, this is a strange misuse of words.*

In Volume 4 he says, "Considering that this Volume was written twenty years ago, none need be surprised to find that some of its statements, although startlingly strong, come short now of the full truth." This is the volume in which he promised the visible resurrection of all the "holy ones of olden time" in 1914. To say that this comes "short now of the full truth" is putting it mildly. One is tempted to ask, *How much farther could it come from the truth?*

WAS MR. RUSSELL SINCERE?

There is a proneness in human nature to maintain and justify an untenable position rather than admit defeat. There may be an unconscious dishonesty in the laboring of a zealot to bolster up a discredited movement. I believe Mr. Russell thought he was sincere. It would have been eternally to his credit if, when his prophecies of visible events utterly failed, he had confessed the unreliability of all his unique interpretations of the Bible. As it was, it was a bitter pill to swallow when the events of 1914 mocked his soothsayings and marked him as the champion wrong guesser of the centuries. Doubtless he was willing to save his doctrines with as little confession of error as possible.

"SCARCELY A WORD"

As already quoted from his foreword in the 1923 edition of Volume 3, Mr. Russell let himself down easy by saying, "Scarcely a word of the volume would need to be changed if written today—twenty-six years after." Whatever Mr. Russell thought of the scarcity of words needing substitutes, *someone did change a great many words and figures, and in the effort to get away from original meanings they went to the extreme of nonsense in some places.* Here are a few samples from Volume 3.

On page 126, "at A. D. 1914" is changed to "after 1914."

On page 228, "before 1914" is changed to "after 1914" in two places.

On page 362, "before" is changed to "near."

On page 364, "must" is changed to "may" in two places, and in a yet later edition another "must" is changed to "may."

As before noted, even the pyramid measurements are changed.

WAS RUSSELL INSPIRED?

In the above mentioned foreword of Volume 2 Mr. Russell says, "This Volume makes no claim to infallibility, and no claim of any direct inspiration from God in the interpretation of His Word." In Volume 3 he says, *"We disclaim anything akin to inspiration* in connection with these Studies in the Scriptures" (italics mine). Unfortunately his confession came after many thousands of people had accepted his teachings as inspired.

In the face of these admissions, Volume 7, the "Posthumous Work of Pastor Russell," is extravagant in claiming all that common people understand by the word inspiration, and more than was ever claimed for any prophet of God except his Son.

Speaking of Pentecost, it says: "The mighty rushing sound represented Pastor Russell's receiving a rich endowment of the Spirit of God" (p. 384). "Many Christian ministers have had a glimpse of the Word of God, knowledge of some details of the Plan, some measure of the Holy Spirit; but to Pastor Russell, God's messenger to the last stage of the church, was given a superabundance of gifts . . . " (p. 385). "In all his warnings he claimed no originality. He

25

said that he could never have written the books himself, it all came from God through the enlightenment of the Holy Spirit" (p. 387). In this volume, written after Mr. Russell died, they say, "The chariots and horses of fire have come for Elijah . . ." (p. 70).

If Mr. Russell had no inspiration from God and no originality, there are not many other sources of doctrine to choose from. When Mr. Russell excused his mistakes he denied his inspiration; when Volume 7 exalts his doctrine, they deny his originality. I accept both denials.

ANOTHER CHANCE AFTER THIS LIFE

When a system of doctrine denies the Deity of Jesus and the personality of the Holy Spirit (Vol. 5, p. 293), you may expect it to belittle the results of sin. I know of no exception. One of the central teachings of this society is that the sinner will have a chance to repent after death. This is reassuring to the sin-lover who wishes to keep on in his sin, and I have no doubt that this is why this system of doctrines so easily wins friends. There is no doubt that false teachers can in every case outbid the offers of the Word of God in their promises of easy escape from the penalty that must follow wilful sin. Let the sinner consider that since Mr. Russell has had another chance after death to "manage every feature of the Harvest work," it is not managed any better than when he lived. Before they rely on his guarantee of salvation after death, let them be sure that his *promises* are more dependable than his *prophecies*.

PROPHECIES CONCERNING 1918-1925

I do not insist that Mr. Russell wrote Volume 7; I merely accept the claim of the book that it is his work. If he did not write it, his successors were guilty of perpetrating a great hoax; if he did write it, then he is responsible for the renewal of the prophecies that failed in 1914. In this Volume 7, the upheavals that were to come before 1914 are set for a period of years from 1918 to 1925. We are assured on page 64 that in the spring of 1918 "the last members of Messiah will pass beyond the veil." Also that "the close of the Heavenly Way" (whatever that is) will be 1921. On page 62 the author is positive "that the spring of 1918 will bring upon Christendom a spasm of anguish greater even than

The "Seven Thunders" of Millennial Dawn

that experienced in the fall of 1914." On page 258 is this dire forecast: "The three days in which Pharaoh pursued the Israelites into the wilderness represented the three years from 1917 to 1920, at which time all of Pharaoh's messengers will be swallowed up in a sea of anarchy." On page 542 is a forecast that a revolutionary movement will be successful in or after 1918, but "not one vestige of it shall survive the ravages of world-wide, all-embracing anarchy in the fall of 1920." As this book was written in 1917, it took a bold prophet to announce that "after 1918 the people supporting churchianity will cease to be its supporters" (p. 399).

ONE FIXED DATE AND EVENT

With all the flux of dates that have come and gone as the end of the forty-year period, the Russellites have never budged from a sure claim that the forty-year "set time" began in 1874. They insist that on that date the Lord Jesus came to earth invisible. At one end of the forty years they relied upon an invisible event, and at the other end of the forty years many visible events. It seems never to have occurred to the many thousand followers that if the claims for one end of the forty years were false, perhaps the other end was in doubt.

EVEN SATAN DECEIVED

It would be unkind for me to originate the statement that these people misled the Devil himself, but Volume 7 implies that very thing. On page 128 it says, "No doubt Satan believed the millennial kingdom was due to be set up in 1915." Now where would Satan get such a notion? The answer is easy: Mr. Russell explains the source of Satan's misinformation on page 612 of Volume 4. He says: "Satan does not possess the holy spirit and is not guided by it, and consequently much of the divine Word is foolishness unto him. But he has learned, no doubt as the world to some extent has learned, that 'the secret of the Lord is with them that fear him.' We may presume therefore that his representatives, the fallen angels, are frequently present at the little conferences and Bible studies, etc., of God's truly consecrated people, to learn something of the divine plan." (Here, as elsewhere, I have tried to quote statements exact-

27

ly as I found them. Mr. Russell calls the Holy Spirit "it" and spells the name without capitals, though he spells Satan with a capital letter.)

HUMAN LIMITATIONS

This is a blundering world. There is much that we do not know about ourselves, much more that we do not know about the mighty span of the universe, and vastly more that we do not know about the infinite Spirit empire that keeps blazing suns on parade. It is enough to stagger the faith of man that such a God of such an empire will make a place in the realm of spirit for man. Glorious Book of God that tells us more than we can yet understand! What a pathetic farce to meet such a revelation with a conceit that makes the mightiest prophecies of that Word head up in Charles T. Russell! Nor is such a conceit limited to one cult.

"MILLIONS NOW LIVING WILL NEVER DIE"

(Title of J. F. Rutherford's book dated 1920)
I am willing.
I have no objection to the millions living now, or any other time, making life permanent. Jesus said, "If a man keep my saying, he shall never see death." If that was what Mr. Rutherford meant, he would have misled no one with his slogan.

His proclamation meant that millions living in 1920 would never experience physical death and he did not make his sinner-pleasing promise depend on any previous conduct or sincerity of the pensioners.

The mischief of the slogan is that it is used to offer a false hope to "MILLIONS NOW LIVING WHO ARE ALREADY DEAD" (Rev. 3:1). Many persons not familiar with the Bible are deceived with his apparent appeals to Scripture because they do not know he juggles with spiritual death and physical death so that one appears to mean the other or both mean neither, as his purposes demand.

The most solemn warnings of God are ignored or twisted out of their obvious meaning to offer comfort to sin-lovers. The God-hater is offered hope just as though the Scripture said, "Whatsoever a man soweth, the opposite shall he also reap. For he that soweth to his flesh shall of the flesh reap unending physical life—soon after 1920."

"THE WORLD HAS ENDED."

This is another slogan in this book.

According to the book, it ended in 1914. That means that it had been ended six years when Mr. Rutherford wrote it and has been ended fourteen years when I write. I must in justice to Mr. Rutherford say that *he and his following have their own private definitions for some words.* World does not mean world and ended does not mean ended. World means "Gentile Times" and ended means it keeps right on after it has "legally" stopped.

There is an old saying, "Where there is *much* smoke, there must be *some* fire." Mr. Rutherford seems to proceed on the theory that where there are *many* words, the public will think there is *some* truth, and the theory seems to work. I have not tried to count the number of times this slogan appears in this one book, but *I have counted 95 appearances on the last 12 pages of the book.*

In a later book, Mr. Rutherford claims for this book a circulation of 2,500,000 in eight months. Counting only the last 12 pages, that puts the slogan on paper 237,500,000 times in eight months. It's a stubborn old world that keeps right on after it has been reminded so many times that it has ended. If the average of the first eight months has been kept up, even if we limit it to 12 pages, the defiant old world keeps on in the face of information given to it on paper in 2,850,000,000 places.

But who cares if by some trick of words or private definitions, this man has ended some sort of world? Let him amuse himself. I would not waste an hour playing hide and seek with his shifting definitions, but for the fact that it is Russellism redated and redressed with a new fig leaf here and there, flagrantly false in some statements.

On pages 85-86, Mr. Rutherford says, "Pastor Russell for forty years pointed out from the prophecies that it [the war] would come in 1914." I wish I might think that Mr. Rutherford said this in ignorance of what Mr. Russell prophecied during the 40 years. I have before me as I write, Vol. 3 of Mr. Russell's books, showing a publisher's date of 1923 and on page 153 it says, "AND WITH THE END OF 1914, WHAT GOD CALLS BABYLON AND MEN CALL

CHRISTENDOM, WILL HAVE PASSED AWAY, AS ALREADY SHOWN FROM PROPHECY" (emphasis mine). In that same volume, in a foreword by Mr. Russell, dated 1916, Mr. Russell says, "... at one time we supposed that the Harvest work would have been fully accomplished with the ending of the Times of the Gentiles. This was merely supposition, which proved to be without warrant..." Mr. Rutherford must know that the Great Pyramid of Egypt was stretched 41 inches to make it fit into a revised prophecy (?) that *seemed* to foretell the date of the war. If he does not know of the excuses Mr. Russell made for his mistakes, I shall be willing to show him.

If Mr. Rutherford does not know that *Mr. Russell's prophecy missed the war by forty years*, we need not expect his "Bible (?) Students" to know much of their own sect.

Surely he knows that Mr. Russell looked for the physical resurrection of "the ancient worthies" in 1914, because Mr. Rutherford himself set the date forward 11 years. Let me quote Mr. Rutherford. On page 89 he says, "Therefore we may confidently expect that 1925 will mark the return of Abraham, Isaac, Jacob and the faithful prophets of old, particularly those named by the Apostle in Hebrews chapter eleven, to the condition of human perfection."

I am charged with persecution because I call attention to these guesses. If *only one* of the patriarchs had come back either in 1914 or in 1925, it would have humbled me, but it appears that *not one* prophet, nor one almanac will pay the least attention to their appointments.

I have found one part of one prophecy of Mr. Rutherford that did COME TRUE. On page 97 he says, "Based upon the argument heretofore set forth, then, that the old order of things, the old world, is ending and is therefore passing away, and that the new order is coming in, and that 1925 shall mark the resurrection of the faithful worthies of old and the beginning of reconstruction, it is reasonable to conclude that MILLIONS OF PEOPLE NOW [1920] ON THE EARTH WILL BE STILL ON THE EARTH IN 1925" (emphasis mine).

Millions living in 1920 were promised five more years!

I am asked why I do not refute the doctrines contained in the billions of pages they have printed. It has been done a hundred times, but what is the use? The man who can know the false prophecies and

The "Seven Thunders" of Millennial Dawn

still believe these people are the sole custodians of the truth about God's plans here and in eternity, evidently *wants to believe it and it is well near impossible to change the want-to in people's lives with argument.* Some parents have found that out.

WHAT IS THE WANT-TO THAT INVITES HERESY?

There are certain characteristics that advertise most false prophets as effectively as a striped pole does a barber shop.

Why is any heresy attractive to people who love to have their own way?

Let the Holy Scriptures answer.

The argument of the first false prophet in Eden amounted to this, You can have more to eat, be better educated and rise to the level of gods. As for this threat of death, "ye shall not surely die."

A wayward people will welcome prophets who prophesy "smooth things," as God says in Is. 30:10. After the false prophets had *told the kings what the kings wished to hear,* the messenger exhorted the true prophet to please speak like those same OPTIMISTS (See I Kings 22:6-13). In Jer. 6:13, 14, God denounces the false prophets who say, "Peace, peace; when there is no peace." In Ezekiel 13:6, the false prophets are described as giving a false hope. In Jer. 14:13, the false prophets are reported to have promised immunity from the wrath of God. Again in Jer. 23:17, the false prophets said, "No evil shall come upon you." In Jer. 27:14, the false prophets promised escape from the penalty for sin. In II Tim. 4:3, the demand for false teachers is foretold in these words, "For a time is coming when they will not tolerate wholesome instruction, but, wanting to have their ears tickled, they will find a multitude of teachers to satisfy their own fancies." (Weymouth's Translation.)

The lullaby-lute of the devil has many strings; here are some of them:

There is no sin; what seems to be sin is only retarded evolution.

You are not to blame for your sin any more than for the color of your eyes.

Sin is not very bad, a little ceremony will give you immunity.

Have a good time now; repent (if you must) just before you die.

If you die unsaved, a little punishment after death and some ceremonies will save you.

Millions now living rely upon some scheme that will swindle Satan and buy heaven with gestures, but no cult has ever appeared more brazen in distorting Scriptures to make it advertise damnation as a side entrance to glory, than the sect that hangs the heaven sign on the hell road.

No matter how much men have "trodden under foot the Son of God," the living and dead are promised a more favorable opportunity to be saved than ever, when "Millions now living" get a chance to "never die."

After hearing the doctrine, a neighbor said to me, "That doctrine suits me; some of us old d——s will never be saved while we live."

Another man whose name belongs to church—who knows more of baseball than he does of the Bible — expressed surprise that these people have Scripture for everything they say. So did the devil have Scripture when he invited Jesus to cast Himself from a pinnacle of the

31

Arguments Against

temple and his use of it was not such a travesty on good sense as some samples of their interpretaions.

Human speech has never been adequate for God to give boundaries to His promises and warnings. In all the Bible I know of no place that language thrills and chills in its effort to fathom God's love and portray His wrath, as it does in Revelation 19.

There are two suppers, one for the Bride and one for the buzzards. In explaining the supper for flesh-eating birds, Vol.7, page 296, makes the birds mean first, "the far-sighted ones, the Little Flock" (Russell's flock, of course). By reading a previous exposition as directed, we learn that five of the kings to be eaten are CREEDS and the author says, "Doubtless the reader has eaten them, in a symbolical sense. They are there to be eaten." The captains to be eaten are religious denominations and he says, "No doubt the reader has eaten them also."

Thus they make piffle of the solemn warnings of God.

Now let us read the 15th verse where language fairly staggers under the burden of God's warning.

"HE TREADETH THE WINEPRESS OF THE FIERCENESS AND WRATH OF ALMIGHTY GOD."

Could human language do more to cool the fever of a sport-mad world?

The author explains it thus, "The Lord assumes an interest in and a responsibility for the complete series of STUDIES IN THE SCRIPTURES, the last one [Vol. 7] of which represents the winepress feature. . . ."

The flippant exposition is that the Word of God in this place records God's interest in completing Mr. Russell's books with this Vol. 7.

Vol. 7, then, is the winepress of the fierceness and wrath of Almighty God.

Words fail me. It is beyond the reach of any language appropriate here.

It is my task to point out the loose ends; it will be for you to answer to your own conscience and God as to what you do with plain facts.

MILLIONS NOW LIVING ARE OFFERED THIS SORT OF STUFF AS BIBLE STUDY!

Thousands now living, not knowing the Bible, take it for granted these people are Bible students *because they give themselves that name.*

Millions now living have bought, found on their doorstep or had given them, this kind of literature not knowing that it is based on the assumption that a large portion of Revelation was meant to describe the performance of C. T. Russell.

Why does God permit it?

Why has he ever permitted false prophets?

I do not know, unless the answer is in II Thes. 2:11, 12, ". . . . . that they should believe a lie: that they all might be damned who believed not the truth, but had pleasure in unrighteousness."

After reading that Mr. Russell was the loud voice of Jesus, we may better understand the prophecy of Jesus in Matt. 24:5-12, "Many shall come in my name saying, I am Christ; and shall deceive many . . . many. . . many. . . many. . . many. . ." MILLIONS NOW LIVING WILL DO WELL TO HEED THE WARNINGS OF JESUS.

32

The "Seven Thunders" of Millennial Dawn

The "Millennial Dawn" people who now call themselves "International Bible Students Association," have sold or given away millions of pages of literature to people who did not know what it really was. Suppose you give some of these books to your Russellite neighbors and see how they like their own methods coming back.

If you wish them to sell, loan or give away, we will send you postpaid, not less than ten of these books or of the ones named below, for half price—provided you have already read the book you order. Not less than ten of a kind for one dollar postpaid.

Other books at same price—20c postpaid.
"Jocko Homo Heavenbound"
"Puddle to Paradise"
"The Toadstool among the Tombs"
"Alibi, Lullabi By-by"
"The Gee-Haw of the Modern Jehu"
"Rastus Agustus Explains Evolution"

HOMO PUB. Co., ROGERS, OHIO

Arguments Against

Arguments Against

THE AUTHOR "GIVES HIS EXPERIENCE."

When I was a boy, I knew (?) more than I do now.

I lived in a world of THINGS and accepted my world for what it *seemed* to be.

My mental equipment passed for knowledge because I made the same mistakes that others did. A counterfeit coin that one *thinks* is gold, will buy as much as real gold if everyone makes a similar mistake.

Once I knew that solid things *are solid* and when my teachers told me that even granite was made up of particles in tremendous commotion, they made it easier for me to believe in miracles. Physicists introduced me to a whirling universe and a world of VIBRATION — sound, light, heat, atomic solar systems, everything in ceaseless motion.

When they crumbled my world into molecules, I reasoned that the molecules must be solid and *stuck together.* When they divided the molecules into atoms and then dissolved the atoms into electrons — smaller than the smallest small things man had before conceived — and these electrons merely whirlwinds of energy, what I had called THINGS turned out to be only the BEHAVIOR of things.

Once I understood (?) time, space, matter, force, gravitation, life, and had hopefully tackled eternity and infinity. After I had been deflated by a philosopher that the world called great, I was willing to know less and let God know more. I offer below some questions like the ones this man asked.

Does time flow past us or do we flow through time? If both flow together, then what is past time or future time? Is the FUTURE a thing before it is PRESENT or is the PAST anything after it has gone? Since even a split second is made up of what has not arrived and what has past, what is the PRESENT?

If a thimble filled with space is moved into a room filled with space does the thimble space displace any room space? Does the thimble have the same space before and after being moved?

If what we call matter is only a manifestation of molecules made up of atoms that are the wrapping paper of electrons that are themselves only imprisoned forces, *what would matter be, apart from force?*

If force is only pulls and pushes, attractions and repulsions that do business with what we call matter, *what would force be in a universe empty of matter?*

Is half of eternity as long as eternity? Unless half of eternity is endless, then must not the other half also have an end, and can eternity have ends?

Can there be infinity times infinity times infinity? One can imagine a line infinitely long; then one may multiply it by an infinite number of imaginary lines to the right and left and multiply this multiplied infinity by infinite levels imagined above and below—why not?

After looking through a powerful microscope at unfathomed depths of detail and through a mighty telescope at unmeasured immensity, who are you, to butt your brains into the biography of God to tell Him what He has done or how He did it?

"The fool hath said in his heart, There is no God." The double barreled fool has said in his logic, "God has done nothing contrary to my reason."

Arguments Against

RASTUS AUGUSTUS EXPLAINS EVOLUTION
By B. H. SHADDUCK

Author of "Jocko-Homo Heavenbound," "From Puddle to Paradise," "The Toadstool among the Tombs," "Alibi, Lullaby, By-By," "The Gee-Haw of the Modern Jehu," "The Seven Thunders of Millennial Dawn" and other papers.

Rastus Augustus, a pompous old colored man, is the college janitor who "listens in" on the class in biology and is aided and abetted by fun-loving students who delight in teaching him theories which work confusion in the colored community, and rehearse him in words and phrases quite beyond his reach.

Mammy Lou, the accepted sage among the women and known in the little colored church as a "Scriptorian," makes no secret of her scorn for any theory that would put the Bible in eclipse. As occasion demands, she works in the home of one of the professors who, not sharing the views of his colleagues, helps Mammy Lou to defend her faith, much to the discomfort of her mate.

Jeff is a visiting nephew who wonders why his uncle is no longer a worker in the church, and Rastus undertakes an explanation.

A PHILOSOPHY OF BUNGHOLES

Rastus cogitates that "guessing" is not a "pedigogical word" and the Bible is not an "educated book."

"I is an evolutionary, I is."

"Uncle Ras, is you all agin the gov'ment?"

"Most emphatical no! I is agin supe'stition. I is agin Santa Claus stories and snake stories and rib stories foah thousan' years old. Science never make no headway long as she haf to be 'sponsible for ever'thing what the Bible specify."

"Is you turned infidel?"

"That ain't no polite word for no college folks; I is a 'vestigator."

"Ain't you believe in no God?"

"I ain't deny no God, but he ain't scientifical; he never got hisself differentiated."

Copyright 1928 by B. H. SHADDUCK

"You mean he ain't done been segregated?"

"That ain't no fitten word for no God. 'Pears like the human fambly need a more or less God, but he is just promiscuous like, same like what you call anonymous. The scientifical p'fessors 'low evolution need a God same like a doughnut need a hole. It ain't a sure-nuff doughnut if it got no hole, but the hole never make no doughnut. The Bible ain't no educated book and man ain't originate from no dust. Science cogitate that God never git hisself scientificated cause he is an abstraction."

"Abstracshum? That don't say nothin' to me."

THE LIKENESS OF AN "ABSTRAC' " AND A BUNGHOLE

Mammy Lou gave vent to her pent-up feelings. "He done tol' you, chile. Abstrac' is anything what soon as it gits by itself, *it ain't.*"

"They ain't no sich thing," said the puzzled Jeff.

"Shore they is," continued Mammy. "Ain't they sich a thing as a bunghole?"

"They is."

"And when you take it away from the bar'l, it ain't. I like to know how this Rastus person goin' to get his evolushum started if he ain't got no sure-nuff God."

"As I was about to say," said Rastus, "Scholar men hypothecate that matter and fo'ce git evolution started when they wrassel and wrassel with each other."

"I like to know," said Mammy, "if your scientificators ever 'scover any matter what can stay by itself without fo'ce, and if they ever find any fo'ce what git lonesome and act up all by itself?"

"Madam," said Rastus, with mock politeness, "you is accidentally approximated what no instructified man deny. Matter and fo'ce project around like one is the inside and t'other is the outside of what nobody exactly understand."

"Then these yere matter and fo'ce is same like bungholes; when either one of them go off solitary alone by itself, *it ain't.*"

Rastus was clearly disconcerted, but he elected to treat the interruption as though he had not heard it. "As I was sayin', 'bout a billium years ago, this matter and fo'ce *combine* [!] in some for-tu-itous way to git *life.*"

3

"Uncle Ras', is that a abstrac' word?"

"That is an educated word what you can't understand," said Rastus, feeling that he had *put his theory over the heads of common critics.*

Mammy was not diverted from the track so easily. "This Rastus man start in with two bunghole abstrac's what he say nobody understan' and now he tote in another abstrac' what nobody got to loan. He bow God out one way and the debbil out the other and stick bungholes together till he spile his pedigree and bust his religion. When he git his bunghole bar'l together, God and the debbil laugh, 'cause it won't hold anything but embalming fluid and posies in his hand."

Mammy had mixed her metaphors till Jeff did not see she was referring to the logical end of brute progeny.

"Co'se a bunghole bar'l wouldn't hold embalming fluid," said Jeff.

"Your uncle will," said Mammy. "This yere miscellaneous god of hissen didn't say, 'let us make man'; it jest say, 'let us make abstractums and then git excused.' When a human critter is jest seven hops ahead of a toad, in this yere evolutionism, he ain't no fitten vessel for eternal life. Rastus got three abstractums now and every time he tote in another, I 'low to make a tally mark on the stove pipe."

"How come you say I got three abstractions?" asked Rastus.

"Does you 'low life keep on bein' life when it separates from what it live in?"

"Mebby not," said Rastus sheepishly.

"Course not," said Mammy, "it jest same like the letter O; when it git its rim knocked off, *it ain't*.

Rastus hastened to escape the logic by reducing life to the minimum and fading it into the past so far that criticism could not follow. "Woman, this life is only a little protoplasm what git alive so long ago, it ain't worth argufying. It ain't 'mount to nothin' 'cause it ain't big enough to make a 'skeeter sneeze if it git snuffed up his nose. It jest a little shadder of something so next to nothin' that the pint of a needle seem same like a ten-acre paster field. It know nothin', see nothin', hear nothin'; it ain't even got a head end and tail end."

"If it got *any* life, it got more than a mountain and *it*

4

would bust up evolution to make it now. It take only one word more to say eternal life. 'Pears like you is mighty persnickery 'bout trinity in the Bible, but you 'low they is matter, fo'ce and life in a little proto-spasm and every one of 'em ain't nothin' *when it git un-trinified.* Resurrection ain't any more miracle than when your hypothecators turn what ain't life into what is life."

"This yere little one-cell feller ain't nothin' atall but a factor," said Rastus.

A STARTER AND STOPPER NECESSARY

"How you goin' to git a factor if you ain't got a factory? How you goin' to git a factory what will make jest one proto-plaster and quit before it makes two? *If it make two, it might make plenty.*"

"Woman, I ain't specify no habit, this yere plasm git alive by *accident*."

"Bunghole four," said Mammy. "Is accident anything before it happen? Is it anything when the thing what it aim to happen to *ain't there when it git there?* Anyhow, if you 'low accidents happen and 'riginate life, you is shore goin' to bust up your evolution, 'cause when you got enough accidents, you got *accidental creation*."

"They ain't no call to originate no life after you git it started. Evolution cogitate *only what it needs*. It don't need no miracles and it tolerate only scientific accidents."

"'Pears like you need tame accidents, else some accident runnin' 'round loose might kill your accidental life. Anyhow, how you goin' to stop gittin' accidental life? 'Pears like you need an accident to happen to your accident so that one bunghole fills up the other one afore you git two kinds of ancestors."

EVOLUTION PROGNOSTICATES BACKWARDS

With a pretended disregard for Mammy's remarks, Rastus addressed himself to Jeff. "It ain't no use for science to argufy agin ignorance. This yere life git alive by *spontaneous combustion*. You got to have a powerful mikerscope to see it, same like it take a mikerscopic mind to assimilate this yere hypothesis."

"Uncle Ras, has you all seen this hippothemus what is so triflin' that it can't make a skeeter bat his eye?"

5

Arguments Against

"Jefferson Lee, you don't understand educated words. This yere hypothesis is same like prognosticate only it's backwards. When you all prognosticate, you tell what ain't, 'cause it's coming; when you hypothesize, you tell what ain't, 'cause it's gone. When Zeke Jonsing display egg yaller on his vest, his wife hypothesize and say, 'Zeke, you been shootin' craps with strange niggers at Slabtown.' How she 'scover this? She know it take money to git eggs. Zeke got no money 'cept he gamble. He don't win 'cept he use loaded bones. Niggers what know him 'zamine the bones. They ain't no strange cullud gentlemen in town; hence and whereas, he 'bliged to been over to Slabtown."

"Or in my chicken coop," said Mammy.

"'Pears like this yere apothesis is same like guessing," said Jeff.

"Your observation is most 'zasperating. They ain't no word more incorrectly dislikable to evolutionaries. Guessing ain't no pedagogical word. When you all put one lone shot in the ole musket and pint it at a rabbit what am precipitate in his momentum, you 'scovers that they is a heap of places where they ain't no rabbit; but when you puts a han'ful of shot in the musket, then the rabbit 'scovers that they is mighty few places where they ain't no shot. One shot is guessin', and a han'ful is hypothesizing."

"Trouble is," said Mammy, "this yere hypotheneuse ain't no ole musket; it's a double bar'l blunderbust and they don't load shot in it. Rastus, he load one bar'l with like-beget-like and t'other with like-beget-different and wad it with hope-sos and happen-sos and can't-help-its and sets traps of abstrac's and missing links and hobble his rabbit with accidents so the critter jest pintedly bound to surrender. Co'se they ain't nothin' what depend more on its legs than it does on its brain, goin' to 'scape such like ambushment, but you deliberate this fact—*if he 'splode his whole ammunition factory, it can't make a rabbit what is, out of something what ain't, and it can't shoot rabbit into some critter what ain't a rabbit.*"

Rastus mopped his bald head with his red bandanna and addressed Jeff. "As I was sayin' when interrupted with highly flippant remarks, this little cell git alive, and it ain't nothin' but stomach, and co'se is bound to grow scandlous fast."

6

Rastus Agustus Explains Evolution

"Where it git vittles?"

"It jest float 'round in the water till it bump up agin other things and jest soak 'em up. Evolution jest need three things, matter, fo'ce and life. No matter how we git 'em, *we got 'em* and they 'splain evolution."

DOUGHNUT HOLES IN DISGUISE

"Rastus Augustus, you is 'most 'zasperating," said Mammy. "You specify you is got three THINGS and nary one of 'em ever been 'scovered bein' a thing by its own self. You is all perked up 'cause you 'low God is abstracshum, but you ain't signify anything else in your evolushum and now you try to sneak in some more doughnut holes."

"I ain't narrate any more abstractions."

"When you got your little proto feller alive, how you goin' keep him alive? First off, you 'low he is *hungry*, but he never find it out less he have an *appetite*. He have to have *instinct* to know what is good to eat, else he might eat pizen ivy or something just as worse. After he git hisself full, he bound to die with colic less he have *digestion*, and digestion do him no good 'less he got *creation* in him to make what ain't alive and ain't hisself into what is alive and is hisself, same like God made Adam. Then you-all certify he is bound to *grow*. Now I ask you if *hungry* and *tastegood* and *instinct* and *digestion* is things that hang around waitin' to git in the first proto when it git here? Moreover, you is bound to have *starters* and *stoppers*."

"How come stoppers?"

PLAYING FROM A HIDDEN DECK

"You 'low it bound to grow, and if it keep on growin' it byemby git so big it make the world lop-sided. You implicate they is a little invisible doodad git alive all by itself by accident and it 'scovers it is hungry when it know nothin' and it hold a collision with something what know less than nothin' and it jest wrap itself around what is scientifical dinner and it don't make mistakes like humans and its dinner is bigger than its diameter and it don't bust its circumference. This evolushum is same like a crooked card game; Rastus start with two aces what he dealt hisself and then he keep fillin' his hand from a cold deck what he got up his sleeve. Now he got a little invisibility *growing* and you

7

watch what he dictate next."

Rastus shifted uneasily and resumed: "When this yere little mite git big enough it begin to pucker in the middle and pucker till it pinch itself plum in two. That's how they come to be two."

ADAM-AND-EVE-ISM

"That don't explain how you keep 'em from gettin' too big," said Mammy. "If they keep growin' it ain't make no difference whether they is one or two, they done fill the world up after a while. How they know when to stop growin' and start bustin'? Rastus have to have just as many stoppers as he have starters and first you know, he goin' to plan another accident and git some other critter to eat 'em up so they don't git too multi-numerous. Now Rastus has to have *bossism* and *puckerism* and *Adam-and-Eve-ism* in this invisible mote of gravy *before he can git two* of 'em."

"I don't participate in your meanin', Aunt Lou" said Jeff.

WHEN SCHOLARSHIP IGNORES THE COMMON HERD

"Rastus can't abide no virgin birth, and he scoff at a piece of Adam growin' into a mate, yet he slip all these doctrines into a little hickey so triflin' that it don't know which end is the other end. This yere little mote of vapor what is so small that enough of 'em to bust up a 'rithmetic can git lost in a smell of noodle soup, can do what Rastus say God can't do with Adam or the mother of Jesus."

Rastus resorted to the oft used plea that scholarship may ignore the common herd. "'Tain't no use to 'spute with 'literate folks what contradic' science. How else we get a population of 'ordial [primordial] germs 'cept they just nacherly dissipate when nature say, 'You is too big to co-operate in one unity'?"

"I been 'specting this *nature* person to git here mos' any time," said Mammy, as she made an extra long mark on the pipe. "I 'low it's been projectin' round with Uncle Sam and John Bull and the Spirit of '76."

"Ain't nature a sure 'nuff real?" asked Jeff.

"Can you measure or weigh or count it? Can you move it or nail it down or find the middle of it? When you 'scover where it 'riginate, if you look close you find the shell outa which Santa Claus hatched."

"Uncle Ras, when these little splasms pucker in two, is one the old one, and t'other the young one?"

"'Co'se not, no more as two ends of a tater cut in two. I seed it my own self in a mikerscope what the p'ofessor show us yisterday, and they ain't no 'sputing it."

"Is the ones you seen just pieces of the 'riginal first one?"

"I 'spose they gotta be," said Rastus, after some confusion.

"Then *the first one ain't dead yet,*" said Mammy, "but Rastus can't swaller Melchizedek stories."

"If they ain't change none in a twillion years, how you 'scover that ever'thing that live come from 'em?"

"As I was sayin', when your aunt start to recite and git me flustered, these protoplasms git so multitudinous many that some 'bliged to starve if they don't git fittings what help 'em swim and fight and swaller, and so some of 'em happen to have a wart or a hair or a wrinkle grow on 'em and now comes the mostest importantest law in evolution—*The fittenest shall survive.* So it come that they is always too many, and the turrible struggle go on, and they get more and more fitten till man git here."

"What come of the ones what don't git no fittings, like you git to see?"

"'Pears like *they is the only ones that sure nuf survive,*" said Mammy. Rastus was trapped, and when they laughed at his confusion he left in a huff. As a parting shot, he said,

"You can't understand evolution onless you want to believe it."

FLAGGING UNCLE RASTUS AT EVERY CROSSING

As he tries to explain how "Protoplasters git fiixins" and other phases of the evolutionary hypothesis

Next day Rastus sought help from the college boys, who rehearsed him in words and phrases calculated to overawe his household. When evening came, Jeff began: "Uncle Ras, when the pro-to-plasters ain't got no fixin's, how do they suddenly git 'em?"

"They ain't no *sudden* in evolution. It take ages to 'velop fins and wings and legs. At first it's jest a hair or a wart or a wrinkle come on the little bag of jelly, and the little feller wiggle it and it 'velop."

"But he got to have muscle to wiggle it, and nerve and brain to wiggle it systematical, and if he ain't got no eyes or nose, he is jest as like to wiggle into trouble as not."

"If you listen instead of scrutinate ev'ry p'int, I can 'splain it."

Mammy made her contribution: "Co'se all these disfigurements on the little plaster is a great hindrance for a thousand years, but this hypothesis say, 'You gotta put up with it, 'cause you is goin' to need it powerful much some day,' and so they stick to it till accidents git to be a habit, and then they can't quit it."

"It's jest as bad as profanity swearin' for your aunt to make fun of heredity."

"I ain't make fun of heredity. Heredity don't turn snakes into birds like you say. Your first little smiggin' don't inherit *nothin'*, and when the east end break loose from the west end they is still orphans. If when they is two ends they ain't inherit nothin', then they ain't help it any to make four ends. A whisker on one end don't inherit to the other end. This educated foolishment made you drunk in your head."

"They is a law of variation go with heredity."

"You say last week that they is a hundred millium times as many one-cell animals as they is animals big a nuf to see."

"They ain't no scholar man dispute it."

"Then your variegated law tech only one in a hundred millium."

Rastus was in a pinch, and deemed the time opportune to unreel his phrase of "educated words," and stun his too critical wife and nephew.

"The exegesis of this [an awkward pause] acclamation of ultimate cogitation specify that the cosmos is invested with circumambient laws what interact between the dictates and the **dictums**."

Jeff's jaw dropped in a reverential way. Mammy was both staggered and disgusted. "When God make the Bible, he don't have to bust a 'rithmetic, beswizzle the almanac, and put the alphabet out of j'int," was her comment.

"Nothin' but shaller minds 'spute what nobody don't

10

deny," said Rastus.

"I ain't 'spute no sure nuf laws. One time you hypothefyers let on that laws is *things*, and 'nother time you act like they is pulls and pushes what make 'emselves without a puller and a pusher. Law is nothin' but words, and if they is real laws they is God's words. *Laws is God Almighty's verbs*, and nature is jest the habit God has of doin' things. I got it right here in Genesis—'And God *said*, Let the earth bring forth the living creature after his kind . . . *and it was so.*' If you got a law of variegation what makes itself and info'ce itself, why don't it git holt of these squidrillions of protomolasses what keep right on bein' protos in spite of all the laws and the asses?"

Even Rastus laughed sheepishly, and answered unwisely: "I 'low it is jest same as white folks' laws: they is some what don't come in the jurisdiction of the co't."

"*That* is jest the p'int," said Mammy. "When you hypothecators git cornered, you git out an alibi or a change of venue, or limit the jurisprudence of the co't."

"Co'se it is oblivious to mental minds, what is used for intellectual pu'poses, that law can't pick and sort where they ain't any variation."

"Ain't you got variation nuf now?" said Mammy. "You tell Tilly's chillun last week that they is a hundred kinds of telescopic germs what float in the air and sleep in the dirt and swim in the mud, and they is jest watchin' to git in 'em and raise a rookus like smallpox and scarlet fever. It wonders me what they had for vittles afore man evolute."

"I ain't hol' no contrac' to 'splain ever'thing at once," said Rastus. "I jest showing' how they is a one-cell life at one end of this evolution and a—"

"Hopeless grave at the other," finished Mammy Lou.

"I git it 'splained if the bystanders didn't all the time throw every switch and flag me at ever' crossin'."

"Never min', Uncle, please tell us how come man," said Jeff.

"As I was sayin', some of these cells don't teetotal pinch in two, but hang together in a bunch like tapioca puddin', and then comes 'nother great law. They change from homoge[n]eity to heterog[n]eity."

Please, sir, can't you say it talk-words?"

"Homoge'eity is when they is one cell what is monoto-

11

nous and all alike. Heteroge'eity is when they is many cells and they is different and 'vide up the work. Same like a first settler—he live simple and do it all, and he is a homogee; but when a lota settlers come to jine him, one say 'I'll be miller,' and another say 'I'll be blacksmith,' and sech like, and they is heretogees, 'cause they foller different trades. When these cells git in a bunch like grapes, some eat and some digest, and some make the wiggles and some do the thinkin', and some *lay the eggs.*"

LAYING HALF AN EGG

"H-m-m," said Mammy, "Rastus done import another shipment of accidents, and yet he say nothin' happen *sudden* in evolushum. 'Pears like these protos got to practice up a long time afore they lay eggs and each generation inherit what their ancestors didn't do and byemby they *almost* lay eggs and byemby after geographical ages, some of the protos lay a half an egg."

"But, Uncle Ras, in the settlement each is a individual. Each one eat and drink and die separate. How can many critters suddenly 'come one critter? How can they change to egg layin' gradual?"

"I can't 'splain it now; evolution got no call to 'splain ever'body's question; *it jest cipher out its own questions.*"

"What do she do next?"

"They ain't no he and no she, 'cause they ain't no sex develop yet. Byemby somehow this heterogeeous feller bust apart, and one part is the pappy person and one part is the mammy person."

"After they quit bustin' apart 'cause it help 'em survive, why do they start it up agin, and if they survive all this time without sex, why do they got to be pestered with it?"

"Evolution *backfires* sometimes," said Mammy.

"Co'se they is inscrutables, but they don't bother hypothesis none, 'cause it figger nothin' can survive 'cept it *do* help. If a thing got to be so, it *is* so. It git you apast what look unreasonable."

"Jest like a sign board say, 'Bridge washed out. Detour'."

"Nary a detour," said Rastus disgustedly. "This is follerin' a trail like a rabbit dog. When the dog lose the trail,

12

he pick it up agin on t'other side of the creek. Same when your mind foller a trail and it come where they ain't no tracks, you stop thinkin' here and resume thinkin' when you find more tracks."

"If they is a thousand years between tracks, it could be another rabbit."

"It's the same rabbit, but he is got a new factor."

"I cain't 'magine how you git a sex factor gradual like. How can it be an *is*, till it is clear past bein' an *ain't*?"

THE ARRIVAL OF A MALEFACTOR

"Easy nuf to git a factor in installments if you got a 'magination factory," said Mammy. "First you git a hypotekettle factor, and then you git a millium years, and then you put 'em in a plug hat and slip in some abstractions, and, hocus pocus, the magic man take a bran' new factor outa the borried hat. Poor little stuck-together cells, they got to be 'sponsible for what their ancestors put on 'em, and they got to inherit what they bust loose from; and if they ain't a nuf factors to make trouble in the world, they got to survive a malefactor."

"Uncle, how these little pa and ma fellers ever 'scover what the plan is?"

Mammy was ready. "The great god Jubiter say to Cupid, 'That little tapioca puddin' that is alive has got pulled 'apart, and they ain't inherit any sex instinct yet, and you better git a supply and go down and fix 'em up, so I won't be delayed none in this terrible slow process of makin' a man. That is one hypothesis; another is that Santa Claus come along and he mistake 'em for a pair of socks, and he put in a passel of laws."

Seeing his uncle ready to quit, Jeff said in a sympathetic tone, "Never mind, Uncle Ras; what come next in this pedigree?"

"We don't mostly know: some say worm; some say it's somethin' like an eel."

"Is they guessin'?"

"You is goin' to spile your sagacity if you all the time is suspicious. When you got to supply evidence what is lost, it is *conjecture*. Ever' time life pass through birth, it put something off and take something on. It's same like a 'spress train start from San Franfrisco, and when it git to N'York

13

we ax the 'spress man, 'Where this train come from?' and he say, 'I dunno, I git on at Jersey City.' Then we look in the cars, and there is a 'Gomery-Roeback catalog wrapped in a Philadelphy newspaper, and we figger it come via Chicago and Philadelphy, but did it come via Denver or St. Paul? One feller say, 'They is icycles on the car, and it been way North, where it is cold,' and another say, 'It takes a thaw to make icycles,' and so each one conject for hisself."

"But how do you reckon it 'riginate in San Francisco?"

"'Cause it spile the hypothesis if it don't."

"This Darwin palaver make me riled," said Mammy. "This 'maginary 'spress train start a billium years ago, without a starter and no conductor and no track laid. When it start it is a thousand times less than nothin' for eyesight to see, and when it stop it is a circus train with Homo the highbrow ape got outa his cage. If the station is where there is birth, then the ole train don't take anything on at the station; it jest drop a splinter off, and the splinter grow into a train, and load up purty nigh ezactly the same as the train it fell off of, and it pass the mammy-pappy train where it has jumped the 'maginary track. Ever'body know brute life begin so small that it's hid in mystery beyond the reach of any mikerscope, and it end in the crumblin dust of death. The only train what ever run on a evolution track end in wreck. They ain't no train despatcher and they ain't no orders 'cept one that Rastus don't own up to: that one is, 'Might makes right; dog eat dog; root hog or die; everyone for hisself and the debbil take the hindmost.' Outa the greed, strife, hate, jealousy, selfishness, cruelty, pain, and death of a billium years man come a crawlin' out somehow. This 'spress train fable of hissen is like a top start spinnin' itself, and when it is spun long nuf, it's a Noar's ark. I can make fables, too. Once they was a man step on a banana skin, and he fall through a worm hole in the sidewalk, and he git up and find he have roller skates on, and he skate right into a pile of shavin's, and bresh hisself off, and his skates is turned to a wheelbarrer, and he git in the wheelbarrer and take hisself for a ride, and he trip hisself up on a hen feather and come home in an airyplane. If Rastus 'low he was a protoplaster a billum years ago and he go on a 'scursion and come in a cattle car and they was monkeys on the train but his folks crowded 'em off, he ain't got no call to

14

fuss about white folks crowdin' him off. Anyhow, I is right glad he ain't no *blood relation* of mine."

"Madam," said Rastus, with a show of wounded dignity, "you insult me when you 'low I is descended from apes. Colonel Darrow and Colonel Cadman say this yere aspersion certifies ignorance, 'cause apes is cousins not ancestors."

NOT APES, BUT REPTILES

"Excuse me, Rastus," said Mammy, with a low bow, "I done forgit that the 'ology book what you brung home, testify that you-all come from reptiles 'way back when they quit washin' theirselves—when they stopped bein' a big word that I can't remember. If you-all 'low you is in the head cage-wagon of a circus parade, I reminds you that some of these days you is goin' for a ride and six men goin' help you out and walk solemn and I like to know if this yere evolutionism goin' git you any wings for your soul to flap when you can't go afoot."

"If your Aunt Lou goin' to preach, I don't 'low to set in the amen corner," said Rastus, as he left the room, shutting the door with more force than was really necessary.

"Jefferson," said Mammy, "your poor old uncle is parrot-ized."

"Yes ma'am, but I don't assimilate your meaning."

"These big words the college boys tell him, done gone to his head. He say what they tell him, same like a parrot. I ain't got enough politeness for his 'varmint'-ism; 'pears like you is the one to sanify [bring to sanity] him."

WHEN LOOSE PLACES GET "HEREDIFIED"

Then come ears and eyes and "sich like," so declares Uncle Rastus on Evolution

A week passed without the subject being discussed with Rastus. Meanwhile, the boy and his aunt had asked many explanations of her employer and favorite professor—the only one in the college who had really weighed the evidence *against* evolution. Before Rastus would continue *his* explanations, Mammy was required to erase her many chalk marks from the stove pipe and promise to restrain herself.

BONES BEFORE THEY GET BONES

"Uncle Ras, explain how come bones to git in critters

15

before any of them had bones."

"First off, they is tough places git in the meat and lime settle there and make bone."

"How come the lime to settle so they is a hole in the settlin's what is closed up at both ends, and grease git stored away in the hollow place?"

"'Cause that's *the scientifical way to make a bone.*"

"How come the lime and tough places can plan it out so they is joints that git themselves made same like hinges only better?"

Rastus only shook his head.

"How you 'spose it come that after the lime and tough places git themselves fixed up and settled down, with a head end and a foot end and a hollow middle, they can grow bigger 'round and longer and git bigger hinges same like they knew ezzactly what is needed?"

"Colonel Darwin say they is some things in-ex-plic-able."

"And when they git broke, they can mend theirselves?"

"Nature is un-screw-table," said Rastus. "When a crawfish git a claw pulled off, it jest grow another one on. The 'ology books certify that they is some critters that when they git broke in two like a freight train, the caboose end grow another engine end and the engine end grow another caboose end so they is same like two trains."

"How come we can't do that? When we git broke in two, do we die 'cause we ain't fittenest to survive or is it 'cause we ain't evoluted up to it yet?"

THE FATAL WEAKNESS OF EVOLUTION

In his perplexity, Rastus, without knowing it, acknowledged the HANDICAP that exists in all higher forms of life —a fact that utterly demolishes the theory of evolution.

"'Pears like evolution work both ways. It bound to see that everything survive that is a survival but it 'low it can't tolerate anything *survive too much,* else it unsurvive everything else."

"Rastus, I offers my congratulashums," said Mammy.

"Woman, your congratulations need scrutinizing."

"How you 'spose backbones git brakes on all the hinges so they don't bend too much and they git a hole through every joint so the telephone cable run through it?"

"Evolution do what *have to be done* and the spinal cord 'bliged to be protected, else the critter git paralyzed."

"How come the critters don't git paralyzed before they git backbone?"

"'Cause the paralysis evolve same time the protection evolve. Neither one git ahead of the other."

"Uncle Ras, how you 'spose nature ever come to think all these plans and contraptions?"

Rastus started. "Where you git that word *think?* Nature don't think. Has your aunt been settin' you up to such foolishment?"

"'Pears like something have to think better than man, 'cause man never ketch up only to the tail end of nature with his thinkin'."

"It jest happen 'cause the fittenest survive."

"Did the ones what didn't git bones all die?"

"*Evolution don't take 'em all.* They is *two kinds* of survivors: them that is fittenest and them that is unfittenest."

"Amen!" said Mammy.

"This ain't no prayer meetin'," said Rastus disgustedly.

"There is *two kinds* of folks git what's a comin' to 'em: them what pray and them what don't," said Mammy.

"Uncle Ras, how you 'spose critters come to git hot blood before anything gits it?"

"'Cause it helps 'em survive."

THEY NEVER ANSWER THIS

"Is a hen survive better 'cause she is hot, than a turtle 'cause she is cold?"

"Jefferson Lee, can't you see the turtle *don't need to be* hot?"

"Did the hen git the need same time she is gittin' the hot?"

"Ezzactly so. I is glad you is scrutinizing that pint. She need to be hot, else how she goin' to hatch her eggs?"

"Why don't she lay turtle eggs what don't have to be hot-hatched?"

"A hen chicken got to be hot 'cause nature *plan* it that-a-way."

"I got to git air," said Mammy, going to the door.

17

"Lots of critters can freeze up plum stiff: and it don't hurt 'em. Do a hen git hot blood so she can freeze up and die?"

"Nature fix 'em up feathers when it fix 'em up shivers," explained Rastus.

"Don't it 'pear like a hen is planned same like mebbe a God would if he was allowed?"

"They ain't no call to meddle any God into it. Fact is, nature make some mistakes and miseries and misfits."

"Mebbe they is a devil gits hisself meddled in."

"Devils aint' needed for mistakes. If they is a devil meddle he can make worse than a mistake."

"Is a mosquito worse than a mistake?"

"Look a-here, boy, you is gittin' too super-scrutinous."

"Uncle Ras, how you 'spect blood git to circumambulating all through the body like a government inspector, and it take along a wreckin' crew and a repair gang and a supply train and a travelin' hospital and a billion soldiers [leucocytes], else when a feller scratch hisself in a berry patch, he ain't fitten to survive?"

"How the blood do so many things is a mystification, but it git circulatin' 'cause first off, they is a hollow place gits full of blood and has cramps and squeeze the blood out. After awhile it *git valves* to hold the blood till it can git another cramp. That's how come a heart, and byemby there gits to be four hollow places and four kinds of cramps."

"When the critter change from three hollows and three valves to four hollows and four valves, does it come gradual like, so it gits three and a half hollows and valves before it gits four?"

"That air question ain't in evolution; hypothesis never git down to cipher in fractions, to answer such like foolishment."

"Uncle Ras, tell us how come eyes and ears and such like."

"'Pears like they is come a time when some little wiggler let his head float outa the water, and he git a freckle or a blister or a sunburn, and it feel different in sunlight as it does in shadder, and so he 'void sunstroke and sickly dark corners, and it help him survive. When it help him survive, he 'bliged to heredify it, all the chillun git it moreso, and after a million years it's eyes."

18

"Heredify?"

"That mean, he make a heredity outa it. Same way they is come a loose place on his head what rattle and buzz when they is a noise, and it gits heredified, and the chillun use it more and more, and it gits to be ears. Same way, voice is a rattle box in the throat."

"How do the little children understand what evolution *aim* for them to git? How they know that byemby it will help their great great grand young ones to have a blister or a wart or rattle box heredified?"

"They got instinct."

"How come instinct?"

"Instinct is jest memory heredified."

HEREDITY WORKS BEFORE IT ARRIVES

"Can they remember they are goin' to get eyes and ears and voice *before* they git 'em?"

Rastus was cornered, but tried a new hypothesis that is hereby referred to evolutionists and "hypothefyers" in general. "I reckon instinct got to heredify what is *goin' to be* memories."

"This yere evolutionism is more wonderfuller to me than a miracle," said Jeff. "It take a sore spot, and make a holler ball, and put it in a socket, and fill it with juice, and make it a lens, and show it how to focus, and make a pucker curtain for it, and fix an overflow drain, and wash it with tears and put it on a universal j'int, and fit a steerin' gear to aim it, and slidin' doors to kiver it."

"Where you git all this machine shop stuff? I was 'splainin' eyes, not automybiles," said Rastus in alarm. "You is purty nigh as cantankerous as your aunt."

"Even if a feller can heredify eyes afore they are eyes, it 'pears to me it would be a heap of botheration to have goin'-to-be eyes before you git sure-nuff eyes. Mebbe evolution plan it out *to have eyelids first,* so they can't any dirt git into the works while they are being heredified into seeing-eyes."

"You hypothecate all wrong, 'cause they is eyes milliums of years afore they is lids."

"How do the heredifyers keep dirt out of them?"

"Dirt don't hurt 'em 'cause they is like fish eyes—*extra powerful tough.*"

19

Arguments Against

"Then when the fish turn into frogs or something that can live on the land, *does evolution make their eyes tender so they can need to keep dirt out?*"

Rastus was puzzled and evaded the question, as some others named "Legion" have done.

"I 'low evolution worked milliums of years ago, so they ain't anyone there to ask fool questions."

This observation was not wide of a great truth. If Rastus had said that evolution-*ists* make their *theories* work in the far past, beyond the range of human experience, where impossibilities are lost in the cracks of geological ages, it would have been both truth and treason.

"Uncle Ras, why don't we see warts and moles and blisters and whiskers turning into new kinds of contraptions now?"

"'Velopment of new organs is so slow that history ain't live long a nuf to ketch 'em at it, but geologers dig up shells and bones and peterfied remains what show that some animals git here after others. The Bible say they is jest created that a way, but science say one kind jest add and subtract a little to a time, and so one kind git to be another kind."

"How many cells did our ancestors have before they began to leave bones?"

"The p'fessor hypothesize that mebbe they had a hundred millium cells before they had sure-nuff bones."

"Then they had to git a hundred million times as big as when they started before they leave evidence for evolutioners."

"Well, what of it?"

"Ain't that a long ways for hypothesizers to hypot before they git any evidence?"

WHAT DO WE GET NEXT?

Seeing his uncle was nettled by the question, Jeff hastened to relieve the situation by offering an answer himself. "Mebbe it ain't size that counts, 'cause insects have more legs and wings than we have and the study books say a fly has 8,000 eyes and a dragon fly has 56,000. Do you reckon that in another million years we will git trigged up with a flashlight like a lightning bug or a spinning machine like a spider or a lot of legs like a caterpillar?"

"You fellers, what make fun of science, is got all you

20

ever goin' to git except brains, 'cause evolution only give you what you can't survive if you don't git 'em."

"But Uncle Ras," said Jeff meekly, "don't 'most everything git trade marks and 'velopments to make 'em look pirty and don't they git equipment so they can help other folks?"

"No, sir-ee!" said Rastus, striking a fist into an open palm. "Where you git that fool nonsense? Colonel Darwin say, if any critter git a 'quipment made to help another kind of animal or for folks to look at, or jest for variety, it 'stroy his doctrine." (Chapter 6, "Origin of Species.")

"Uncle Ras, it 'pears like every bug and bird and beast on earth, except 'varmints,' is helpin' something else same like they is in partnership. The bee carry pollen for the flowers and the flowers call 'em with pirty colors and pay 'em with honey. The plants breath off oxygen what they don't want and the animals say, 'That's jest what I need and you can have a big word what is pizen to me.' The groundhogs dig holes for the rabbits in the summer-time and the rabbits keep 'em open and ventilated in the winter-time."

"That ain't prove nothin', 'cause when critters git 'velopments they git 'em for their own selves *first*."

"Do it help the cat to wobble his tail so the little birds see he is goin' to jump, or do it help the hawk to make a squeal-noise so the birds and baby rabbits hide?"

"Evolution 'low that every 'velopment what don't help critters to survive, help 'em 'cause it gits mates for 'em."

EVIDENCE OF DESIGN

Jeff took from his coat pocket a box containing a beautiful sea shell, a chrysalis of a butterfly marked with colors of burnished gold, a bird's egg marked with a unique design, and a small caterpillar as resplendent with plumes as the cavalcade of a king. "Uncle Ras, how do such pirtyments help them to survive?"

"Mebbe it help 'em git mates."

"They don't git mates, and anyhow, the fellers what live in the sea shells is blind."

"I ain't read up on it," said Rastus doggedly, "but it 'bliged to help them somehow."

"Don't you think the little white spots on the out corners of a robin's tail are just because God want everything

21

different?"

"No sir! Them spots come 'cause when the birds mate they choose mates colored up jest how they like 'em."

"Do you have two evolutions—one to pull and another to push—like when a freight train goes up the grade, they have one engine to pull and another to push?"

"What you all mean with that fool question?"

"'Pears like you 'bliged to have two evolutions—one to go ahead and make the birds hanker for spots and another to come along behind pushin' the spots."

"Boy, they is somebody been a settin' of you up to such foolishment."

"I craves to ask a question," said Mammy meekly.

"You may inquire, unless it is uncompetent, irrelevant and not proper cross-examination," said Rastus with a flourish.

"You say that critters never git any contraption unless it is ezzactly what they need their own selves."

"I answers yes in the affirmative."

WHO WILL ACCEPT THE CHALLENGE?

"Can you name any kind of contraption that man could think of or God could make that evoluters wouldn't claim it came 'cause it helped the fellers what got it? I dare you to specify any kind of contraption a critter could have that God ain't already put it on something."

Rastus was discomfited and the situation was becoming tense, when Jeff renewed the discussion and enabled his uncle to ignore the challenge.

"Uncle Ras, it ain't so much what birds and beasts have that helps other ones, as it is *what they lose or what they ain't allowed to git,* that helps the others."

"Does you meditate that evolution help one kind of critter by taking something away from another one?"

"I allude that somebody see to it that evolution (or whatever it is) ain't allowed to overdo itself."

"'Pears like you postulate that everything ain't allowed to git all the evolution it can hold."

"S'posen the hawk raise sixteen babies and the quail raise two? S'posen they is one proto-feller outa all the squintillion of 'em 'velop into a big bird, fast as a pigeon, with quills like a porcupine, and claws like an eagle, and smell like

22

a skunk, and appetite like a crow, and pizen like a rattlesnake, and it swim like a duck and lay eggs like a tater bug; how is anything else goin' to survive? If all the birds had an appetite for seeds instead of worms, won't the worms multiply and 'vour ever'thing?"

"They ain't none of your fool s'posens in evolution. Nature jest see to it that *everything git to survive* and they ain't no such thing as double survive. Science narrate that some kinds of animals can't keep up with evolution and they get extinct-ified."

DO PARASITES KEEP UP?

"Uncle Ras, do chicken lice keep up with evolution, and did the great monsters in the Natural History book, go extinct 'cause they couldn't keep up?"

"I tell you nature regulate everything so that this is a tol'able like world to live in," said Rastus with a display of irritation.

At this labored effort to ignore the evidence of an over-ruling God who holds evil in check, and substitute some impersonal fictional authority that men call "nature," Mammy said softly, "Oh fools, and slow of heart to believe all that the prophets have spoken."

"Look-a-here, ole woman, if you got to set the Scripter up agin hypothesizers, I got a question to ask you."

"Suits me. We'll ask questions turn about."

"How do animals git from Ameriky to Noar's ark and back agin?"

"Cain said (Gen. 4:14), God has driv' him from the *face* of the earth. That Scripter make out they is some places ain't *face*. Noar gits orders (Gen. 7:3,4) to save seed on the *face* of the earth. God ain't told us yet how things happen on the back of the head. Now I ax you, if little germ-bugs can drown and freeze up and dry up and blow away, and live *anyhow*, how do it help 'em to git giblets and hot blood and a thousand places to have a misery in, and if your religion is the survival of the fittenest or the *fightenest*, what for you complain if white folks tromp on Negroes and survive 'em? You evolutionaries 'mind me of Abe Swayback what steal a little pig of his neighbor and then complain scan'lous 'cause the ole sow foller him home."

"I didn't 'gree to answer speeches; now I ax you, if you

23

Arguments Against

don't like evolution 'cause it's cruel and selfish, how you 'splain why your God plan a world that a way?"

"He never plan it so. Genesis 6 say he is grieved in his heart and sorry he made man and beast 'cause all flesh had corrupted his way. When God have his way, the lion git an appetite for straw like an ox. Now I ax you if it help a gobbler to survive to have ugly red meat-beads on his bare neck to git hurt when he fights, and have a paint brush on his crop and a red snake tail hangin' down apast his nose? Do it help a snake to have a rattlebox on his tail? Do a rowdy ruffian struttin' rooster survive 'cause he dress to be seen, like a target, and crow in the middle of the night, so every varmint in a mile can locate him? Do a flea have pizen itch in his bite, so he can make friends? If a queen bee and the drone bee don't work, how do they hereditate work into the chillun that ain't like neither one, and how do work bees pass on variations what help 'em when they got no babies? You say man is cousin of an ape, 'cause they cut on the same pattern. I ax you how could God make a man so as he don't have any plan, and God has used every plan they is in makin' critters? Anyhow, if man is beast like, it ain't no wonder, 'cause God say he has *corrupted* his way. Maybe a magician can put a fried egg in a plug hat and take out a white rabbit, but your divlution can't take a wart and blister and hives and seven-year itch and make legs and eyes outa 'em, no more than you can grow feathers on a mud turtle in a million ages. It's jest a barnyard religion—"

But Rastus had escaped.

THE ESCAPE OF A SHEEP

If Rastus is a lost sheep, he "don't sheep-blat," says Mammy

As is usual with the purveyors of false doctrine, Rastus showed ten times as much zeal in disturbing the church as he had formerly displayed in building it up. One evening the colored pastor called at the cabin to discuss with Rastus the obsession that had so fired him with zeal. Rastus met him at the gate much as a high school senior greets a freshman, only that his air of superiority was tempered with a generous determination not to be too severe with the parson.

"Pa'son, it is about time you is lookin' after your sheep

24

what git away."

"Are you getting away?"

"I have done escaped."

"From what?"

"From supe'stition and whale stories and miracle yarns and folkslore."

"If you have escaped *from* all these, what have you escaped *to*?"

AS FREE TO SPEAK AS A PARROT

"I has escaped to freedom *in my mind*. I is free to think my own thoughts and I ain't have to follow in the mental feetsteps of tradition. I has got the new 'lightenment and I don't tag along after what my pappy and mammy say, but speak what I think out of my own head."

"Are you freer than Jesus, who said, 'I have not spoken of myself; but the Father which sent me, he gave me a commandment, what I should say and what I should speak'?"

Ain't I allowed to think out things for myself?"

"Rastus, will you tell me just one thing about your new freedom that someone has not told you?"

"I-I 'low your question is not proper cross-examination."

"Perhaps not. I withdraw the question, but the college boys are having fun, believing they are using you to peddle evolutionary theories among the colored people of the community."

"Colored people need the truth to make 'em free."

"Colored people were freed once in the days of Lincoln, only to discover that without a saving faith, mere physical freedom may be dangerous. There is no slavery so hopeless as the shackles forged by misused liberty. How will it help negroes to resist temptation, if you prove to them they are the children of the ape?"

"Hold on, pa'son! Hold on! I hopes you will 'scuse me for amplifying your sagacity, but scientifical people long ago remonstrate that man ain't come from no ape. Man descended from a 'pithecus."

"Do you deny that teachers of evolution have gotten their names in the Sunday papers by teaching that the negro came from a different kind of ape and more recently than the white races?"

25

"I never heard of such stuff. I 'low to ask—I mean I deny it. That jest some white man's *insult*."

"Yes, it would be an insult if applied to but *one* race, but white people consider it a mark of progress to accept animal ancestry, if it is far enough back. Here is a picture of a 'graven image' called 'The Chrysalis' that was unveiled in the West Side Unitarian Church in New York City. I paid that same church one dollar for it.* As you see, it is the figure of a man coming forth from a gorilla. It is true that the sculptor adds a statement that not knowing just what the ancestor of man was, he chose the gorilla for symbolical sculpture because it 'has more in common with man than any other anthropoid ape'."

Rastus tried to laugh off the conviction that somehow he had been insulted and said rather vigorously, "That doggone church done evolution more harm than good. *It's scientific to talk about animal kin-folks but it's an insult to make pictures of it like it happened sudden.*"

THINNING OUT THE INSULT

"It seems, then, it is an insult to picture a man as though he came from an animal in *one* generation."

"I would hit any colored man who say I come from an animal even in twenty generations."

"*Then evolution is an insult if it works too fast.* Rastus, if you are really free, I congratulate you, but how long can you keep what you call freedom? The papers tells of a hundred or more convicts in a Western penitentiary who overpowered their guards and barricaded themselves in the dining room of the prison. *Is that the kind of freedom you enjoy?*

" I ain't 'low to git in no prison," said Rastus uneasily.

"You are under sentence of death."

"Same like everybody," said Rastus relieved.

"Let me give you a fable," said the pastor.

A FABLE OF FREEDOM

Two crows were feeding in a barn lot. One was a tame crow and tame is sometimes a word to describe captivity. The other was a crow from the tree tops and clouds that came to hobnob with his barnyard neighbor.

---

*The author possesses such a picture.

26

Rastus Agustus Explains Evolution

"Tell me your experience," said the tree-top crow.

"My name is Jim Crow. The god of this farm took me from my nest when I neared the age where crows try to fly. Already I feared that I might fall out of the nest and break my neck when the wind blew a gale. He who rescued me said, 'Poor Jim Crow, you are burdened with too many long feathers, I will set you free.' One by one the kind man cut the long feathers in my wings. Really, I had never used them, and they were long and dragging and clumsy. Since then, it has been so easy to flap my wings and keep them clean, that I greatly rejoice in my freedom. Moreover, I am as fat and as well sheltered as the Brahma hens. Now let us have your story."

"My name is James Crow. I have known hardship and sometimes hunger. My parents taught me from the first that there were many places that were not safe places for crows. Indeed, this is one of the places, but now in my mature months, I see that you are safe. My parents must have been old fogies. Now that you remind me of it, I remember that it was hard work to lift myself into the air with wings when my craw was full and I must get back to the tree top on the mountain. Many times the winds buffeted me as I beat my way against them. I have noticed that when the dew was on the meadows, my wings were wet and bedraggled because of the long feathers. Really, I envy you your freedom."

"Why not live on the ground with me?"

"Could I do that?"

"Certainly, but you must give up your hankering for the clouds. The god of this world—I mean this farm—will not suffer you to remain here unless you conform to the fashions of this w-farm. You must have your wings clipped; *that is the circumcision of the world*—on this farm."

"Might I not keep *some* feathers so I can fly when trouble comes?"

"You cannot and be consistent. If you elect to live a barnyard life, do not be divided in your allegiance; if it is good now, it is good all the time. Some of the hens try to be half and half—part of the time on the ground and part in the air. They only get a few feet in the air and usually get into their master's garden and before the dog gets them out, they lose many feathers they would like to keep, besides los-

27

ing the respect of all."

"Shall I be in good company?"

"Indeed, this is a ranch of highly advertised thoroughbreds."

"I am with you in mind; how shall I go about it to enjoy your freedom?"

"You use your mouth to hold fast to that brier and I will use my mouth to pull your flight feathers."

Thus it came to pass that the crows had great liberty—after a fashion.

Now this barnyard was on the banks of a river called "Jordan," that overflowed its banks once a year.

Not many days after, the flood came and the knoll on which the crows were feeding soon became an island with the water rising fast.

James Crow lamented and said, "Oh that I had kept *some* of my feathers," then would I flap hard to rise.

"It would do no good," said Jim, "for the lowlands are covered with water and the mountain is far and you are heavy with dunghill corn."

"Alas! I see it all now. What surprises me is that a *crow* could be fooled so easily."

"Is you-all aimin' that fable at me?"

"You bartered your faith for a temporary freedom; 'How wilt thou do in the swelling of the Jordan'?"

"Pa'son, I don't reckon God will be hard on a man jest 'cause he is scientifical."

"The wisdom of this world is foolishness with God."

"What difference is it goin' to make when I die, if I have descended from animals?"

"I know," said Mammy, "it say in the Book, 'Thou must go to be with thy fathers'."

Rastus *looked* a severe rebuke at her and resumed, "Ain't the shepherd bound to hunt up the lost sheep 'until he find it'?"

"Rastus, are you *lost* or *escaped*?"

"Well, pa'son, I ain't blat much to git back like a lost sheep do," acknowledged Rastus.

"That is a most important p'int," said Mammy. "Rastus don't sheep-blat; he go about rooster-crowin' how free his barnyard is."

The pastor admonished Mammy kindly, and this mollified Rastus somewhat.

"Ain't everybody a lost sheep what ain't in the flock?" asked Rastus.

"Suppose it is something in the flock scattering the flock; is that a sheep?"

"Pa'son, you is rubbin' it in, ain't you?"

"Is a lost sheep a happy sheep?"

"No he ain't, pa'son."

"The same shepherd who told us about the lost sheep also spoke of wolves and He gave another parable about dividing the sheep from the goats. He said, 'If ye were my sheep, ye would hear my voice'."

Mammy could restrain herself no longer. "Is a sheep belong to the shepherd unless the shepherd git his wool? That's a p'int worth scrutinizing."

No one answered, and she continued, "Is he a sheep if he go projectin' around with the inside of a menagerie?"

"Now, Mammy Lou, let us be generous," said the pastor.

"Excuse me, pa'son, but it do 'pear to me like the shepherd won't say, 'Rastus is my black sheep even if his four fathers [forefathers] is a 'pithecus and a marsoop and a lizard and a toadfrog'."

"'Scuse me, Rev'rend, I got some work I is done 'bliged to do at the college. I hopes you will call again," said Rastus with a meaning look at Mammy as he left.

RASTUS JOINS THE A. O. Z.

And Takes an Extra Degree

Rastus had a horror for reptiles of any kind and he was much disquieted that even a book so unscientific as he deemed the Bible would promise a return to his ancestors. As soon as occasion offered, he took counsel with his student patrons and they were eager to add to his uneasiness. After consulting with a concordance, they read to him from the Book, "He shall go to the generation of his fathers," and assured him that generation meant the beginning. They very freely exaggerated the oriental doctrine of reincarnation and unanimously agreed that according to the eternal fitness and science of things, it was logical that any man who failed

29

to live a perfect human life must go back to the beginning—perhaps on some other world—and start again. They confided in him that it was a secret among scientists that this was the only hell that would be practical and was in reality the purgtory that is misunderstood by many.

"White men," said Rastus, "if that air is scientifical, I 'low to walk more circum-spectable. I speculate that I is 'bliged to jine the meetin' house again."

Highly entertained by Rastus' fears of a possible association with reptiles and "varmints" in the future, the boys hatched a plan to further entertain themselves by initiating the old man into a fake secret order that they decided to call the A. O. Z. (Ancient Order of Zoo.)

To this proposition, the old negro objected that it was not "fitten" for a colored man to mingle thus with white folk, but they argued away his scruples by insisting it was a vital doctrine of the order to have samples of each branch of work that evolution had wrought. Besides, they assured him, he could master the details and later be the founder of a colored lodge of the order.

Not far from the dormitories, there was an old building used by these students for a club house and this was chosen as the place for the ceremonies. If there is any limit to the lengths that college boys will go to stage a joke, it has not yet been discovered. It was decided to give Rastus three degrees ending with a grand climax. For this occasion, the boys spared neither brains, labor nor expense, and various disguises to represent animals were borrowed, rented or bought. For the third degree, they secured from the museum several stuffed reptiles of various sorts and borrowed from someone a live alligator not yet half grown. The first two degrees consisted chiefly of horse-play with Rastus dressed in a fur suit resembling a gorilla.

After the second degree, they sat down to a feast while a committee put the finishing touches on the arrangement of another room for the third degree. The plan was to usher Rastus into this room blindfolded and seat him on the floor facing the alligator and flanked on either side by stuffed snakes, a huge turtle and a skeleton suspended from the ceiling. They understood very well that when the bandage was removed, his departure would be precipitous, and to delay his leave-taking, they plentifully covered the floor with banana skins. To add to the confusion, they filled some washtubs with tin pans, broken dishes, a few more stuffed snakes and a small quantity of sneeze powder. These tubs were placed on top of high step-ladders set to collapse on slight provocation. It was planned that the boys would stand near the door to block the exit, trip the ladders and cry out as though frightened and so add to the pandemonium. One tub in falling was to pull a string and fire a gun that in a closed room would be deafening. The final act was to catch poor Rastus as he fled from the building, and quiet his fears.

Now it turned out that when Rastus was seated by the alligator ready for his debut as a full member of the zoo, a sentinel, posted outside, gave the alarm that college authorities had discovered the lights in the building. As the boys fled in the darkness, one of them pulled the electric wires loose from the building and left the rooms in darkness. When Rastus freed his eyes from the bandage his guide cautioned him to sit still until the danger was past and the boys would return. Panic begets panic, and one frightened boy adds to the fear of another, and no boy thought of returning that night.

Rastus, in his gorilla make-up, stretched himself on the floor and was soon in a deep sleep, and with no one to disturb him, he slept late. When he opened his eyes, he saw before his face what appeared to be a very real snake coiled to strike. As he rolled away in terror, he rolled onto the alligator. Gathering his feet under him, he made a wild leap to escape the new horror, but landing on banana skins he skidded into a step-ladder and brought the wreck upon his prostrate form. If his heart had been weak, he must have died then, but with the strength of madness he came out of the ruins like an explosion, headed anywhere to get away. Again the banana skins denied him traction and he plunged head first into another stepladder, bringing on another rain of pots and pans and the roar of the gun. Crazed with fright and seeking only to escape a convention of horrors, he made a flying leap for the window, carrying the sash with him into the sunshine. Down the street toward the colored settlement, chased by dogs and urged on by the screams of women and children who had gathered about a peddler's wagon, he finally reached his own cabin one jump ahead of the dogs and dropped on the floor. Mammy Lou, mistaking him for some unnamed monster, threw the teakettle of boiling water at him but fortunately missed him. When the crockery began to rain from Mammy's direction, Rastus dove under the bed until he could make her understand it was Rastus.

"Rastus Augustus, what has happened?" said Mammy, beginning to doubt her senses.

"I is all chawed up with 'varmints' and dynamited and pizened and scared to death," said Rastus.

Before the college authorities could probe the matter, the boys had cleared up the debris and had bribed Rastus to keep silent, adding to the bribe the exhortation that he was pledged not to betray his lodge brothers. As an added inducement, they promised him that they would regard him as having taken one more degree than had ever been experienced by any member of the order.

Notwithstanding all this, Rastus is uneasy about the purgatory the boys have "hypothesized."

Note: Years ago, the author witnessed a performance something like that described above. In that case, it caused a drunkard to take the pledge *and keep it*. This was a fortunate ending of a dangerous piece of folly planned by a company of young men. The author knew of another initiation of which he was not a witness, that had fatal results, and he solemnly warns any who may read this, to discourage dangerous jokes.

Here are cover designs of three recent books by Mr. Shadduck. Together, they contain 23 cartoons. The book on Russellism has already caused a sensation. These, or any mentioned on page 2, are sent for 20 cents each, postpaid.

HOMO PUB. CO., ROGERS, OHIO

Rastus Agustus Explains Evolution

HOMO PUBLISHING CO.
ROGERS, OHIO

Arguments Against

PAGES FROM
LATER EDITIONS

8TH EDITION   **PRICE 20 CENTS**

JOCKO-HOMO
HEAVENBOUND
BY B. H. SHADDUCK, PH. D.
AUTHOR OF
"PUDDLE TO PARADISE"
"THE TOADSTOOL AMONG THE TOMBS"

SCIENCE? RELIGION? FOLLY?

Before you bring "railing accusation" against this picture-parable of "modernism," consider that it portrays what passes for both science and religion with many people.

There was recently unveiled with solemn ceremony, in a New York "church," a "graven image" called "The Chrysalis." Since satan imitates sacred things, it might better be called "The Modernist Madonna." It is the image of a youth coming forth from a gorilla. Since these "worshippers" profess faith in some sort of heaven, the artist has added what is presumed to be the next stage of evolution and BEHOLD THE FOLLY OF IT ALL!

BEFORE THE PARADE STARTED

This squat "ancestor" with doubtful table maners, is presumed to be the dam or sire of the race. When we found "it" in a magazine this crude poem of our pedigree was only about three drops of ink removed from glorious manhood. They called it "Scientific Symbolism." Elsewhere, this hairy poem is called all sorts of names ending in "-pus." When "Mother Goose" scientists fix up a poultice like this, they OMIT the DETAILS. I have asked the artist to add the brutal facts that put a "D" before evolution. The Bible says, "He that sitteth in the heavens will laugh." no wonder!

Genealogically speaking, the sub-gentleman (center) and his "cousins" are said to have been in the *same hide* when our "ancestors" wiggled loose from the shell of a reptile's egg. After continuing as the *same sprout* on the family tree for some millions of years, there was a split in the family and the more refined learned to use a club and eat the neighbors. According to Theistic-evolution-ism, this was the fortunate beginning of a two-million-year carnival of bloodshed, treachery and cannibalism that would evolve a man who could make the next jump — to angel level — in thirty minutes. Meanwhile, "science" has discovered enough difference between the peace-loving branch of the family and the killer branch to justify keeping one in a cage and letting the other buy the peanuts.

To keep you from being snobbish about it, they say that before you were born you passed through the monkey stage a few days before you reached human exclusiveness. Believe it if you wish, but to me, the wide range of man's capacity for saintliness or deviltry argues that man FELL from God-likeness rather than CLIMBED from reptile level. Science, with all its speed, cannot lift the highest ape to the level of a baby's prayer in a million years.

ILLUSTRATED PARABLE. A certain drum-major of infidels went up from Freethinker's forum to Christian-Money Seminary and fell among foragers who stripped him of his anti-miracle leadership, his reptile-ancestor priority and his ape-cousin exclusiveness. They robbed him of his fund of jokes about Bible stories and plagarized every alibi he had for inspiration. And he said, "If you capitalize my inventions. I shall be a "back number". If you take my monopoly, take me." But they cast, him out *because he was an infidel*, leaving him nothing that is his very own, but circulating marriage and birth evasion. How long will he retain the leadership of that parade?

Puddle to Paradise

By B. H. Shadduck, Ph. D.

Copyright 1925 by B. H. Shadduck

Puddle to Paradise

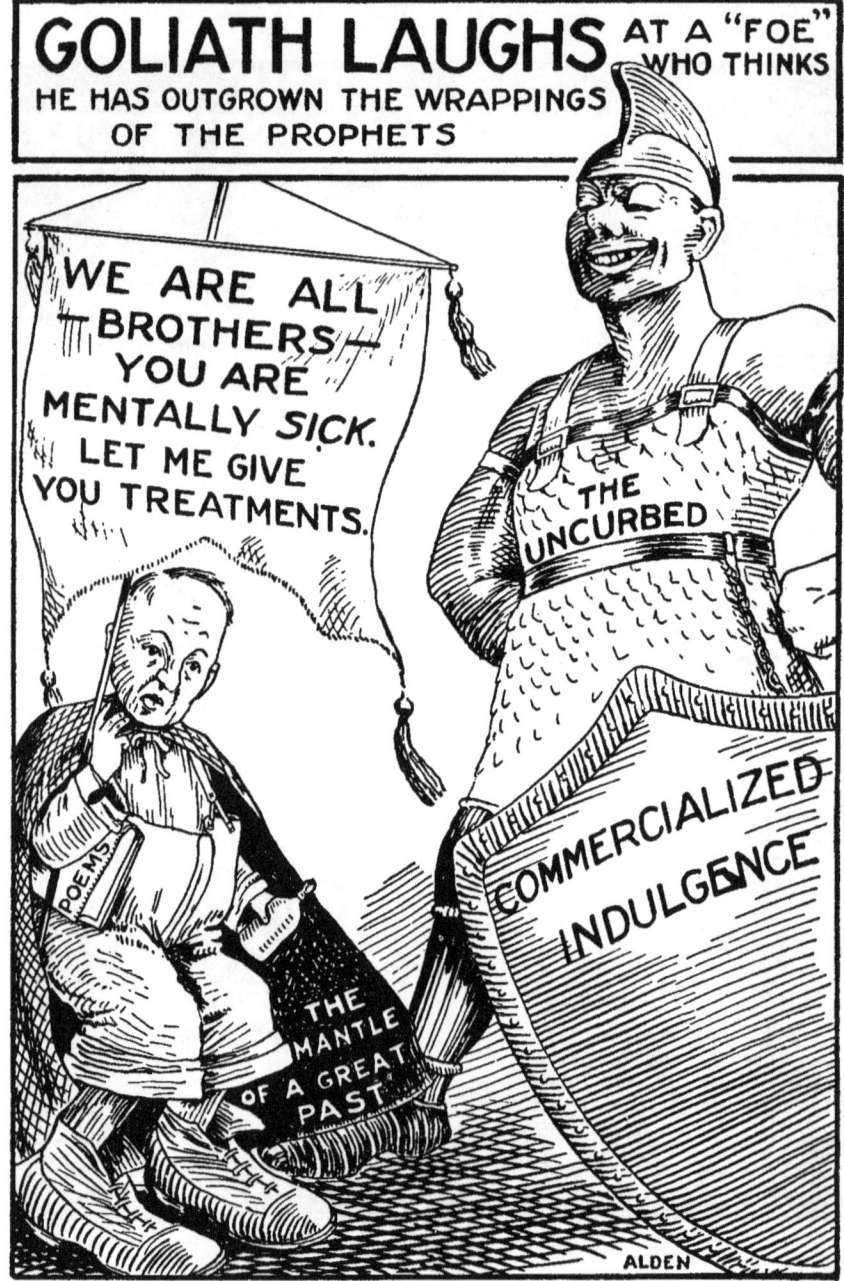

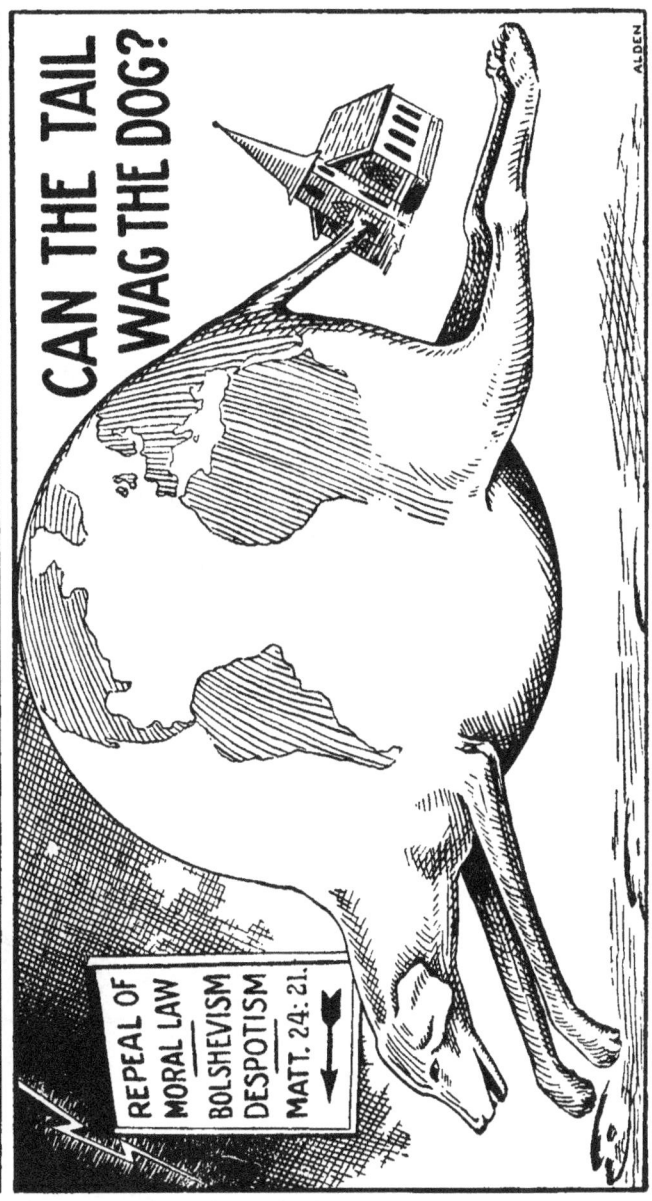

LIGHT OR SATELLITE

No church can be the "Light of the World" (Matt. 5: 14), if it asks the World what it may believe. The tagging church "rethinks" its doctrines to keep up with the parade. Certainly it is not unhitched from the World. James 4: 4.

CAN THE TAIL WAG THE DOG?

REPEAL OF MORAL LAW
BOLSHEVISM
DESPOTISM
MATT. 24: 21.

This sketch portrays the course of many lives, and nations may make the same mistake. There are 3 kinds of liberty—freedom from sin, freedom from troublesome sinners, freedom to continue our kind of sin. Heaven has two of these freedoms; men will die for two of them, but *they are not the same two.*

The "Seven Thunders" of Millennial Dawn

THIRD EDITION   PRICE 25c

The
SEVEN
THUNDERS

OF

MILLENNIAL
DAWN

THE BACKGROUND OF
"JEHOVAH'S WITNESSES"

The "Millennial Dawn" people who now call themselves "Jehovah's Witnesses" have sold or given away millions of pages of literature to people who did not know what it really was. Suppose you give some of these books to your Russellite neighbors and see how they like their own methods coming back.

If you wish them to sell, loan or give away, we will send nine books of ONE KIND for $1. Smaller quantities at 25c each, postpaid. For larger quantities, write for prices. These prices may be changed if cost of materials, printing, or postage is considerably increased.

OTHER BOOKS LISTED BELOW,
at same price.

"Jocko Homo Heavenbound"
"Puddle to Paradise"
"The Toadstool Among the Tombs"
"Alibi, Lullabi By-by"
"The Gee-Haw of the Modern Jehu"
"Rastus Agustus Explains Evolution"
"Mistakes God Did Not Make"
"Dust and Deity"
"Man, The Harness Maker"

HOMO PUBLISHING CO., ASHTABULA, OHIO

Additional Copies of this book
can be purchased from

http://www.lulu.com

GB Graphics is committed to preserving interesting
and unusual materials of the past and putting them
back into publication.

www.ingramcontent.com/pod-product-compliance
Lightning Source LLC
Chambersburg PA
CBHW032037150426
43194CB00006B/312